Desert, Jungle and Dale

The Sebastopol Cross

Desert, Jungle and Dale

A memoir by
Philip van Straubenzee

THE PENTLAND PRESS LTD
EDINBURGH CAMBRIDGE DURHAM

First published in 1991 by
The Pentland Press Ltd.
Brockerscliffe
Witton le Wear
Durham

ISBN 1 872795 12 9

Typeset in 10 pt Times by
Print Origination (NW) Limited, Formby, Liverpool L37 8EG
Printed and bound by
Antony Rowe Limited, Chippenham, Wiltshire SN14 6LH

For my late wife Imogen, my daughters Henrietta and Joanna and the British Officers, Warrant and Non-Commissioned Officers, and The African Rank and File of the Royal West African Frontier Force who fought with me in Somaliland, Abyssinia and Burma (Kaladan) during World War II, 1940–1945.

If you can talk with crowds and keep your virtue,
Or walk with Kings – nor lose the common touch,
If neither foes nor loving friends can hurt you,
If all men count with you, but none too much;
If you can fill the unforgiving minute
With sixty seconds' worth of distance run,
Yours is the Earth and everything that's in it,
And – which is more – you'll be a Man, my son!

Rudyard Kipling

Acknowledgements

It is almost invidious for me to select particular individuals for thanks since I have enjoyed such invaluable help and advice from so many quarters. Nevertheless, I must make the attempt in the hope that my memory will make the list of benefactors comprehensive. To avoid tiresome repetition or variations on the 'my thanks' theme, I therefore propose to name each person concerned, with a note on the cause for my gratitude.

My brother Henry. We have always had a close relationship, and in addition to commenting on the manuscript, he has helped immensely with much of my reminiscence for the first twenty years of my life especially.

General Sir Anthony Read. A lifelong friend of my own Regiment, who served with me in both Abyssinia and Burma, and whose comments on my manuscript in the early stages were invaluable. Sir Anthony provides the Foreword to this book, and has also contributed the account of our safari together, as young lieutenants, in what were then little-known parts of Africa.

The Editor of *Yorkshire Life* (Mr. Maurice Colbeck), for permission to include Ronald Harker's colourful article on the Sebastopol Cross and the brief history of the van Straubenzee family which forms the introduction to my memoirs.

Mr. Louis Allen, the author of *Burma: The Longest War*, for advice in the early days of planning this book.

Mr. Brad King of the Imperial War Museum, who helped greatly with the production of wartime photographs of the campaigns involved.

Mr. Peter Clark of the Royal Geographical Society for meticulous research touching obscure place names for the campaign maps, and Mr. David Ward for producing excellent maps of the Battle of Waddara and our West African safari.

The late Mr. George Kinear, formerly War Correspondent of the *East African Standard*, of whose graphic stories I have made full use.

Battalion Headquarters Staff of the 1st Sierra Leone Regiment of the Royal West African Frontier Force: my Second-in-Command, Major Bill Dawkins; my Intelligence Officer, Captain Peter Clements; and my Signals Officer, Captain Tony Matthews. These Officers have contributed materially to the Kaladan story.

Friends who have commented on and contributed to the manuscript at various stages: Susan Viscountess Mountgarret; Joanna and Gerry Farrell; Professor Jim Jeffes and his wife Hope; Captain Humphrey Thornton-Berry, Canon Frank Ledgard; Mrs. Rosemary Marston, Lt. Colonel Peter Wade and Mrs. Helen Wrightson (who also describes our motoring holiday in Austria, Italy and Corfu in June 1982); and Mrs. Miranda Armitage (who is responsible for the diary of our Art Study Tour of Russia in 1983).

Major Jeremy Whitaker, Mr. I. A. Irving and Mr. Digby Angus for highly expert advice on the illustrations, and the reproductions.

Her Majesty's Stationery Office for permission to reproduce the map entitled 'The Battle of the Lakes' from the Abyssinian Campaign.

Mrs. Lynne Moore for kind permission to reproduce her beautiful watercolour painting of Spennithorne House and Lower Garden House.

The Countess Pralormo, who has, graciously, provided a photograph of her husband, the late Major-General Count Pralormo, Commander of the Italian 24th Division which opposed us so gallantly and tenaciously at Waddara.

A reproduction of the excellent portrait of myself painted by Mr. Gerald Leet in New Delhi in 1946 has been chosen for the front cover of my memoirs.

Captain Bunny Nash, Mr. John McGavin and Mr. Eric Lanning, with whom I have been in constant touch for advice and research throughout the preparation of my memoirs. They served with me in differing campaigns in East Africa or Burma, and have provided me with valued photographs and memorabilia.

Colonel Bill Gordon, Signals Officer of the Gold Coast Brigade, for authoritative advice on the Abyssinian Campaign.

Mrs. Anthea Walker for so patiently, neatly and accurately typing and retyping my manuscript material again and again over a period of six years.

Mr. Laurence Cotterell for bringing his long publishing experience to bear on my project, with comments on the contents of my memoirs, and advice leading to the conclusion of a satisfactory agreement with the publishers of this book, the Pentland Press.

Sir William van Straubenzee for counsel and assistance in updating an extract from his grandfather's book on the Family Record of Service with the Armed Forces.

Mr. Anthony Phillips and Dr. Pamela Grant, my Editors at the Pentland Press, who have been most understanding and co-operative in making the production and publishing of this book so smooth and trouble-free.

CONTENTS

FOREWORD

by
General Sir Anthony Read, G.C.B., C.B.E., D.S.O., M.C.

I have known the author of this book since 1934. Our paths have crossed frequently and for long periods. We were brother officers in the 43rd Light Infantry, went to West Africa together, and have served there, initially in the same battalion; we were both adjutants of battalions in the same brigade on mobilization, and both commanded West African battalions in the same brigade in the Burmese campaign. Later, as a divisional commander I lived next door to Philip in his Yorkshire village. And so, for me, it is an honour and a great pleasure to be asked to write the foreword to his autobiography. It is also rather difficult, as reading his text has made my memory work overtime, and of course my memory has not recorded things exactly the way his memory has done. That has produced a slight urge to nit-pick, which I hope I have managed to resist.

He was a gallant officer, and a worthy successor to his military forebears. He has told the story of his military experiences in a thoroughly factual and modest way. I had thought I knew him fairly well, but this book discloses an inner turmoil which I had never suspected, which has taken much strength of character to overcome, and which made difficult some of his personal relationships with authority. He led a West African battalion, with distinction, through the second Kaladan campaign in Burma - and this was a battalion experienced in jungle warfare - and he was NOT - and who were all strangers to him when he arrived; the African soldiers of this battalion came from a different country, and were quite different people to those he had experienced before. This was no mean feat of leadership. Earlier he had been adjutant to a somewhat difficult commanding officer throughout a period of complicated and confused fighting in Abyssinia – Philip contributed in a big way to keep the battalion running smoothly, and achieving the fine result it did. Little has been written about the magnificent performance of the West African soldiers in the appalling conditions of the fighting in Abyssinia and Burma. It is good to read their praises here, praises which are in no way exaggerated. I was there, and know exactly how unpleasant it was.

He loves his Yorkshire home, and this theme runs through his story. The countryside, the land, the shooting, the home and the cricket, are all vital anchors to him, and gave him the courage to endure when personal tragedy struck. This book reveals to us a gallant soldier, no great brain, a great lover of his Yorkshire home, who has lived an honourable life and done much to uphold the high standards of his family and regiment.

List of Maps

List of Illustrations

FAMILY PHOTOGRAPHS

Introduction

If you stroll through the parish churchyard at Spennithorne, near Leyburn in North Yorkshire, you are almost sure to note a curiously-wrought gilded cross which stands out like a commander in a regiment of orthodox English gravestones. It is odd but appropriate, for the cross is a battle trophy.

The clue to its origin is in the church itself: an oil painting of a golden cross toppled from a church roof in Sebastopol. How it came to Spennithorne is an episode in the military history of a family whom the fortunes of war brought to Yorkshire from Germany via Holland in the early days of the eighteenth century.

Philip William Casimir van Straubenzee, born at Tournai (now in Belgium) in 1723, followed his father into the army. But, bored with garrison duty in Holland, he got leave from his commissioned service in the Dutch army to join Hessian troops. The Hessians came to England under treaty obligation in 1745 to help defend the kingdom of Hanoverian George the Second on the eve of the second Jacobite rebellion. He was billeted at Guisborough, near Kirkleatham. There he fell in love with Jane Turner, the daughter of wealthy parents at Kirkleatham Hall, and twelve years his senior. They were married at Acklam against the wishes of her family, and in 1746, when the Stuart cause had been finally lost at Cullodon, he took her back to Holland.

But Yorkshire had got into his blood. He resigned his Dutch commission in 1748 and returned to England. He was naturalized by Act of Parliament in 1759 and settled down to farming (it is thought) first at

Kendal and then at Kirkby Lonsdale. And there he died in 1765 at the age of 42, having fathered three sons and one daughter. Thus the English van Straubenzee family was founded. The military tradition Philip had inherited continued unbroken.

Almost 100 years later Philip's great grandson, Charles Thomas van Straubenzee (later General Sir Charles), was in the Crimea commanding units of The Buffs, the 31st Foot and the 72nd Highlanders. On the last day of the siege of Sebastopol he was hit in the cheek by a bullet while in action at the head of his brigade. After eleven months of siege the Russians had given up and shortly afterwards the gilded cross was on its way to surmount the family burial plot at Spennithorne, where Sir Charles's great-uncle had purchased an estate.

Nearly another century later Sir Charles's great-great-nephew was leading African troops against the Japanese in Burma. By a pleasing circumstance his Christian names are a modern link of those of the romantic couple who began the English family descent, for he is Colonel Philip Turner van Straubenzee, D.S.O., of Spennithorne House.

Chapter 1

Early Days

My own story starts in South Africa where, in Johannesburg, I was born in 1912.

My father, Henry Turner van Straubenzee, came of a great North Yorkshire military family and he was the only male in twenty-two generations not to have served in the armed forces of the Crown – he was an extremely successful civil engineer working for C.A. Parsons of Newcastle and he met and married my mother in South Africa when he was working for his firm.

My mother, Elfreda Rogers, was both charming, very good-looking and a very strong character. She was one of a family of thirteen, the daughter of a British South African businessman, W.M. Rogers, and was born and brought up in Cape Province.

Sadly, my father died of typhoid at a very early age leaving my mother to bring up myself aged 2 and my brother not yet 1 year old.

I was now the prospective heir to the small Spennithorne Estate in North Yorkshire and my grandfather, the present owner, was anxious for my mother to bring us back to England to live with him and my grandmother at Spennithorne.

It was a considerable ordeal for a young South-African-born lady to leave her home with two small children for a totally new life in the United Kingdom's Yorkshire Dales with two elderly in-laws, but this decision was hers alone and we arrived at Spennithorne two weeks before the outbreak of World War I.

It is a long time ago now but my recollections of my childhood at Spennithorne were very happy ones.

Small incidents, trivial perhaps, come to mind, Christmas at Constable Burton Hall (two miles) when Mrs. Wyvill, step great grandmother of the present Squire, Charles Wyvill, sent her carriage to fetch us, the weekly ride in the donkey cart to Harmby with the washing.

Henry and I had a governess, Miss Parker, very mean she was, a bowl of milk every day for breakfast meant for us but 'Parkey' scooped the milk out of the bowl and kept the cream for herself!

These were the years of World War I and with two uncles involved; one on the Western Front in the Royal Horse Artillery, who commanded the Rocket Troop and subsequently the Chestnut Troop, survived in spite of being wounded twice or three times and getting a D.S.O. and Bar. The other in the Royal Navy was Gunnery Officer on H.M.S. *Good Hope*, Admiral Craddock's Flagship which was sunk with all hands at the Battle of Coronel in November 1914, casting sadness and gloom at Spennithorne.

Looking back on those early days at Spennithorne – the staff consisted of three maids and a butler. There was no central heating so there were coal and wood fires in all the rooms including the bedrooms. There was no electricity so the house was lit with oil lamps and candles. The housekeeper's room, now my kitchen, and the servant's hall were both actively being used in those far-off days by a large staff.

There were two gardeners, John James and Fred Clarkson, father-in-law and son-in-law. My brother and I spent all our time with them, that is to say all daylight hours, when we were allowed to do so. Fred had lost both an eye and a leg in Flanders, but he still was a well-known bowler in village cricket in Wensleydale. He bowled off a very long run, for one with a wooden leg, but he made the ball turn sharply from the off and got a lot of wickets. My brother and I were fascinated to watch him taking his false eye out and cleaning it.

For us, the excitement of the Summer was hay-time, when John and Fred used to cut, with scythes, the small field in the garden to provide hay for the donkey in the Winter. The donkey was harnessed up to a small cart which had high wooden sides fitted in hay-time, and was otherwise used for garden work, or taking the family washing to an admirable laundress in the nearby village of Harmby. My brother and I thought that riding on top of either the hay or the laundry was the nearest approach to heaven that two small boys could get.

My grandfather, in spite of crippling arthritis, used to go for quite long walks with one or two sticks. He, like his youngest son, had been a

Horse Gunner, and had commanded the British Artillery at the Battle of Tel-el-Kebir in 1882. On one of his walks, to a high point near his own property which looked over the whole of Upper Wensleydale, he met the village blacksmith, Willie Metcalfe, who had been a farrier in a cavalry regiment in Flanders. Willie told me this story years later: he said, 'Your grandfather said to me, "Metcalfe, I know I should not say this, but look up the dale to Middleham, look at its church and castle, what a wonderful artillery target"!'

In 1920, my mother took my brother and myself for a year's holiday to South Africa where we stayed with my other grandmother at her lovely house at St. James, near Cape Town. My recollections are of a lovely climate and bathing and surfing on the Musembergh beaches.

We returned to Spennithorne two weeks before I was due to start my schooldays at Aysgarth (four miles from Spennithorne).

I could not say that my earliest days at Aysgarth were happy ones and the headmaster of the day (Frank Joy) described me as the unhappiest boy that he had ever had!

Later on when we were both at Aysgarth, we were invariably asked to stay with some extremely generous elderly second cousins either at their home at Batheaston just outside Bath, or in Scotland where they took a house and property with sporting facilities every Summer. Wherever it was, there was always an immaculately mown lawn with a cricket net, and Henry and I were bidden to report at, say, 10.30 a.m. for cricket practice. Cousin Willie had been no mean cricketer, and appeared in well-pressed white flannels and a Free Forester blazer, with at least five buttons down the front, and demanded to be bowled at. I doubt if either of us ever hit his wicket. He was a brilliant shot and I remember on several occasions seeing him kill a left-and-right at snipe. These were happy holidays, and we accepted, I hope, with good grace what seemed to two early teenage boys the imposition of changing into a black tie and stiff shirt for punctual dinner at 8.00 p.m. when we could on occasions have been fishing for sea trout by moonlight.

As time went on, I began to enjoy life and found that I was good at all three games, and in particular cricket - there is no doubt that in those days, games took a high priority and I failed to get into both Wellington and Marlborough, due mainly to the fact that I considered games a higher priority than my work.

I was lucky eventually, due to my Aysgarth headmaster, Frank Joy, to have been accepted at Sherborne School, Dorset, and here again, I disliked it, and was enormously unhappy. My four years at Sherborne were undistinguished - my only success was five credits in my School Certificate which resulted in almost total idleness for two years subsequently, and failure in my first attempt to pass into Sandhurst which in those days was almost unheard of.

My brother and I were very keen cricketers at school, and in later years, and we looked around from about the age of 16 for holiday cricket; too early to belong to the Clubs, but not too early necessarily for village cricket, particularly in Yorkshire. At that time Spennithorne only had a football club; so we settled for Cover Bridge. No village, just a fishing inn on the River Cover, but able to draw on cricketers from nearby villages, Middleham, Leyburn, Finghall, Danby and others. The Captain and organizer, and owner of the cricket field, was an extremely good-natured eighteen-stone Yorkshireman, Landlord of the Cover Bridge Inn, called Dick Stott.

My brother and I called on Dick early one Summer holiday, aged perhaps 15 and 17, and offered ourselves for Saturday afternoon cricket. The offer was accepted at once, and we had some splendid seasons. The ground was literally a small square surrounded by barbed wire and wooden posts, which had to be removed just before a match started. Cattle grazed on the rest of the field and remained *in situ* during a match.

The Cover Bridge ground lies midway between the River Cover and the River Yore and the distance to either River from the actual wicket was comparatively short.

Sixes into either River was the order of the day and much time was lost in retrieving the ball but it was all great fun. A local squire, who lived further up Wensleydale, claimed when playing for his local village against Cover Bridge, to have killed a salmon in the Yore and a trout in the Cover, by hitting sixes into both rivers. I don't think anyone believed him.

Most other village cricket pitches were similar, and one, without cattle, was a hayfield in the recognized season. If a ball was hit into a hayrick the batsman was entitled to keeep running until the ball was retrieved. From memory nineteen runs was the record. It was all very good natured and comparatively light-hearted.

On one occasion when Cover Bridge were playing a village called Crakehall in an evening match, in early September, homeside Crakehall were short of three players, but took the field with three Cover Bridge substitutes. We (Cover Bridge) had made a respectable score by 5.00

p.m. and declared, at which precise moment three figures appeared in sporting clothes, the headmaster and two assistant masters of the nearby famous Preparatory School, Aysgarth, where Henry and I had been educated. The Crakehall Captain fell on them and, with no discussion or even approval from Dick Stott (the Cover Bridge Captain), had no difficulty in persuading them to fill in the three vacant batting places for Crakehall. Tommy Thompson, the Headmaster of Aysgarth, was a well-known cricketer locally – he played for the Yorkshire Gentlemen and Harrow Wanderers, and in spite of having walked up partridges all day with his two colleagues, between them they succeeded in hitting off the runs with pads over plus fours to ensure victory for Crakehall. One or two black looks, side-long glances, and the occasional 'booger that for a game' and we repaired to the local pub for beer at about 7.00 p.m. with absolutely no lasting ill will.

Looking back, I believe the reason for my dislike of Sherborne was the complete lack of encouragement I received on the games front, particularly as I had left Aysgarth with a big reputation for both cricket, rugger, and soccer.

Failure in my first Army exam resulted in my leaving Sherborne and plans being made by mother for me to go to an Army crammer for a second attempt.

I well remember that period of my life and being unsure whether I really wanted an army career. However, some family pressure was placed upon me, particularly in view of the exceptional record of the van Straubenzee family for service in the armed forces.

The crammer chosen for me was at Camberley – its name Holmdale and the principal tutor a Mr. Tinniswood. Holmdale was a pretty 'sleazy' establishment, the classrooms as I remember them were corrugated tin sheds, gloomy, dark and cold. There were about ten of us students, mostly 'dropouts' from famous public schools and all first-time failures for the Army.

The tutors were low grade and rather than teach the subjects required were persuaded by us to give talks on 'sex' and other topical subjects.

Tinniswood himself was an experienced and high-class teacher, extremely adept at forecasting questions which might be asked in an Army exam. He proved right and I passed reasonably well into Sandhurst, but not before we had an abortive attempt to burn the Holmdale classrooms down!!

After a long holiday at Spennithorne I entered Sandhurst in the Winter term of 1929 – one's first term at Sandhurst is an ordeal and I found it a rough, tough existence. I found myself in No. 1 Company in the new buildings and the first morning is etched in my memory. We were paraded in pitch darkness on the Company Parade ground with C.S.M. Pratt (Grenadier Guards) and two other Staff Sergeants screaming at us and then marched into Camberley to fit uniform and footwear.

Life for the first few weeks consisted of endless drills (square bashing) and cleaning leather belts, scabbards and boots.

The spare time, although limited, was very happy and I made friends for life.

Daily programme at Sandhurst was extremely tough and energetic and in one single morning we could be confronted with periods of drill – P.T. and equitation – I could not say I enjoyed the equitation period – I was, and am, an indifferent horseman and consequently in the bottom 'ride'. I well remember our Staff Sergeant Instructor, Staff Sergeant Guinavan, an Irishman, who disliked me together with an Indian Cadet Nazir Ahmed and three Chinese Cadets, Shei, Hu and Lin, and he delighted in calling out our names and placing us on either the most sluggish or alternatively the most frightening of the horses in our ride. One horse, Blackcock, with fire in its nostrils and a wild look in its eyes, used to take me over the hurdles in the Riding School at breakneck speed, ending frequently in a heavy fall.

I took part in all games and sports at Sandhurst but probably my best achievement was to box for the past against the present, although losing on points in a long and 'bloody' contest.

My intermediate and senior terms were uneventful and I was promoted to the rank of Corporal in my final term and passed out in the Summer of 1931.

Sandhurst in the 1930s was a considerable mental and physical test in stamina, but the recreational interludes were happy. Cadets were ruthless and rough with anyone who did not conform with a set and recognized standard of behaviour and the punishment was severe: all clothes stripped off and a run down to the Lake (300 yards) – a plunge in the water and a run back all the time followed by a yelling horde.

Towards the end of my Senior Term, I was interviewed for my first and only choice for Commissioning into an Infantry Regiment. It was to the Oxfordshire and Buckinghamshire Light Infantry, with Peter Young who subsequently became a lifelong friend, that we presented ourselves in front of the Colonel of the Regiment Major General Sir John Hanbury Williams (affectionately called Hanbury Banbury in the Regiment).

Chapter 2

Peacetime Soldiering

Both myself and Peter Young were selected for this Regiment, the 43rd/52nd, and we began an army career at Bordon Camp, Hampshire in September 1932 – Martinique Barracks was a pretty grim place in those days, huts constructed of corrugated sheeting and bitterly cold in Winter.

I recall that early days in the Regiment were pretty lonely, brother Officers very seldom spoke and clearly wanted to have a good look at newly joined subalterns before being accepted into the Regimental family.

Soldiering between the Wars was very easy going, particularly during the Winter months. All Company Officers attended Company office at about 9.00 a.m. when minor offences were dealt with by the Company Commander. We then all used to repair to the Mess for mid-morning drinking.

The afternoons were almost entirely given up to games of every description.

The 43rd was very much a 'horsey' Regiment and hunting was encouraged – Company Office was invariably attended in hunting clothes.

It might seem from reading the above description of life in the 43rd that it was 'play' and very little 'work'. However, in those days, there was a manning system, i.e. trooping in the Autumn to keep our Overseas Battalion (52nd) up to strength and that left the 43rd very short of soldiers during certain parts of the year – gradually the Regiment filled up again with recruits until moving overseas at the next Trooping season.

After six months, life to me became much more enjoyable – I got to know and like my brother Officers.

In those bygone days we were able to hire the Regimental chargers for hunting or drag lines and I became extremely keen on a weekly gallop with the Bordon Drag in the Hampshire countryside. This was a tremendously exciting half-hour's ride over a different piece of country each week.

I had one fearful fall sustaining concussion and a broken wrist and spent three weeks in the Cambridge Hospital.

The Summer months were full of activity. There was always a month of Battalion and Brigade Training on Salisbury Plain or Tidworth and sometimes we were required to take part in the Aldershot Tattoo, where I rode a Regimental Charger 'Coldstream' at the 'Battle of Omdurman'.

There was splendid cricket at Bordon and many of the 43rd Officers played both Regimental cricket and also for the Bordon Garrison that had fixtures with many of the well-known Clubs.

In those years 1935–1940 we were entertained to some lovely country-house cricket at the home of Reggie and Michael West, Alscot Park in Warwickshire. These were halcyon days, large and lavish house parties.

I sustained a rather unfortunate accident during those days at Bordon. At some roughish fun and games in the Mess, a friend and brother Officer, Firpo Ward, sprayed the contents of a tin of 'Sprinko' into my right eye. 'Sprinko' was a very strong disinfectant used for cleaning baths and not good for the eyes! It did not do my eye much good and I was partially blind for some weeks and in considerable pain. Time was the great healer and after a period of 'double vision' I became completely cured.

Firpo is still a great friend and over 80! During the last year at Bordon, I became very keen on hockey and, playing in the Regimental Team, we went a long way towards the Army Championship. I had had enormous fun with my old Charger 'Gone Away' and rode him finally in the Regimental Race at the South Oxfordshire Point-to-Point, managing to come in fifth.

The Regiment moved to Colchester in 1935 and it was here that I became unsettled and bored with soldiering in England and together with Tony Read (afterwards General Sir Anthony Read) we decided to apply for Secondment to the Royal West African Frontier Force.

The Colonial Office selected us for appointment to the Gold Coast Regiment and in 1936 we embarked in the Elder Dempster Line M.V. *Accra* bound for the Gold Coast.

My impression of that first passage to the West Coast was not good.

The boat was full of hardened 'old coasters' and there was heavy drinking from almost after breakfast until late at night. I was homesick and missed my friends in the 43rd.

We landed at Accra in heavy surf and were met by the Adjutant 1st Gold Coast Regiment (Lieutenant Hutchinson), a kindly man who did everything to make us welcome.

I can't say that I enjoyed my first few months on the 'Coast' - it was frightfully hot, a wet heat, and believed in those days to be the 'White Man's Grave'.

It had earned its name from its high incidence of malaria, black water fever, sleeping sickness, yellow fever and Dengue fever, to name a few - and on our arrival on the coast little had been done to eradicate these horrors.

We worked from 6.00 a.m. until 8.00 a.m. when it was comparatively cool - after breakfast we did a short spell of office work then a long siesta followed by lunch and a variety of games including golf, cricket and polo in the cool of the evening.

The Gold Coast soldiers were great fun to work with - their living quarters were basic and simple, a grass hut where each man lived with his wife or wives and children. I made many and lasting friends.

Polo was tremendous fun and we played twice a week mainly with our own Gold Coast Officers, Police and a few civilians.

'Six Feet' was the name of my pony which I also entered in the Accra Races, being unplaced.

About this time, I and other friends in the Gold Coast Regiment had been considering plans for a fairly lengthy safari in parts of West Africa unknown to us.

General Sir Anthony Read (already mentioned, then a Subaltern Officer like myself) has produced an account of this memorable journey covering remote areas of British and French West Africa (a diagrammatic map of our route is shown on page 13).

> 'In the somewhat leisurely way of life in the Gold Coast Regiment before the war, one was entitled to take some local leave, in the middle of one's eighteen months' tour. I think we were allowed three weeks, not long enough to go home, or go to South Africa (no passenger flying in those days) - But what to do? Philip, Alan Boggis and I thought we must be mildly enterprising, and see a bit more of West Africa. We planned a trip that took us from Tamale in the North of the Gold Coast down to the coast near Accra: thence by road through Togoland and Dahomey and into Nigeria; north from the Nigerian coast to Sokoto and then out into French colonial territory to Niamey, on the river

Niger, which was the starting point of the weekly trans-Saharan bus service which ran somewhat irregularly in those days. Then south again through Ouagadougou and back into the Gold Coast at its north western corner, and so back to Tamale having done a round trip of something over two thousand miles. We found a willing chap who hired us his nearly new Ford truck very cheaply (and he himself as mechanic), packed our kit and supplies, and set off in a very lighthearted way. We were not explorers, but we were slightly more enterprising than many of our colleagues. The route I have outlined was a rough track, or desert track, no comfortable tarmac surfaces, fairly indifferent maps and endless ferries over the many water obstacles near the coast, each ferry appearing more rickety than the one before. We took with us our personal African servants, and we camped each night, or slept in government rest houses, in some comfort. I have happy memories of sitting round a camp fire, eating stew (it was always stew) which the 'boys' had prepared, under a magical starry African dark velvet night sky. We were self-contained for basic food, but of course bought vegetables, fruit and eggs (occasionally not too fresh) as we travelled. On our journey we had passed through the thick forests of the centre of the Gold Coast and Nigeria, the open country near the coast near Accra, the orchard bush and Savannah leading up to the fringe of the Sahara. We had encountered many different African tribes: the Arab type of Fula and Touareg in the desert, the Mohammedan northern warlike tribes of the northern states, the forest dwellers and the coast people: all very different types.

Looking back fifty years, I think we were very fortunate. We were none of us ill (although we were traversing the White Man's Grave), we had no disasters, the truck never broke down, we didn't get arrested, although we photographed everything of any possible interest in French territory. And we got paid for our journey. We took a bit of care, and put together a fairly detailed route report of our travels in French colonial territory and the intelligence world rewarded us with a cheque which just about covered the cost of hiring the truck. And of course, above all, we had a lot of fun, had seen lots to interest us, and we had all learnt a great deal.'

One incident which I call to mind and which General Tony omitted to include in the excellent description of our three-week African Safari in 1937 was whilst *en route* in Upper Volta or Niger districts, the road suddenly ceased and below us we came upon a deep chasm where presumably a bridge had once been in existence.

This was clearly a major calamity as there was no possible way round this obstacle: however, the native population generously came to our assistance and two long steel girders were produced and laid across the gorge. On this rather unstable and rickety bridge we made a successful but somewhat adventurous crossing.

A picture of our truck and intrepid African driver (I believe his name

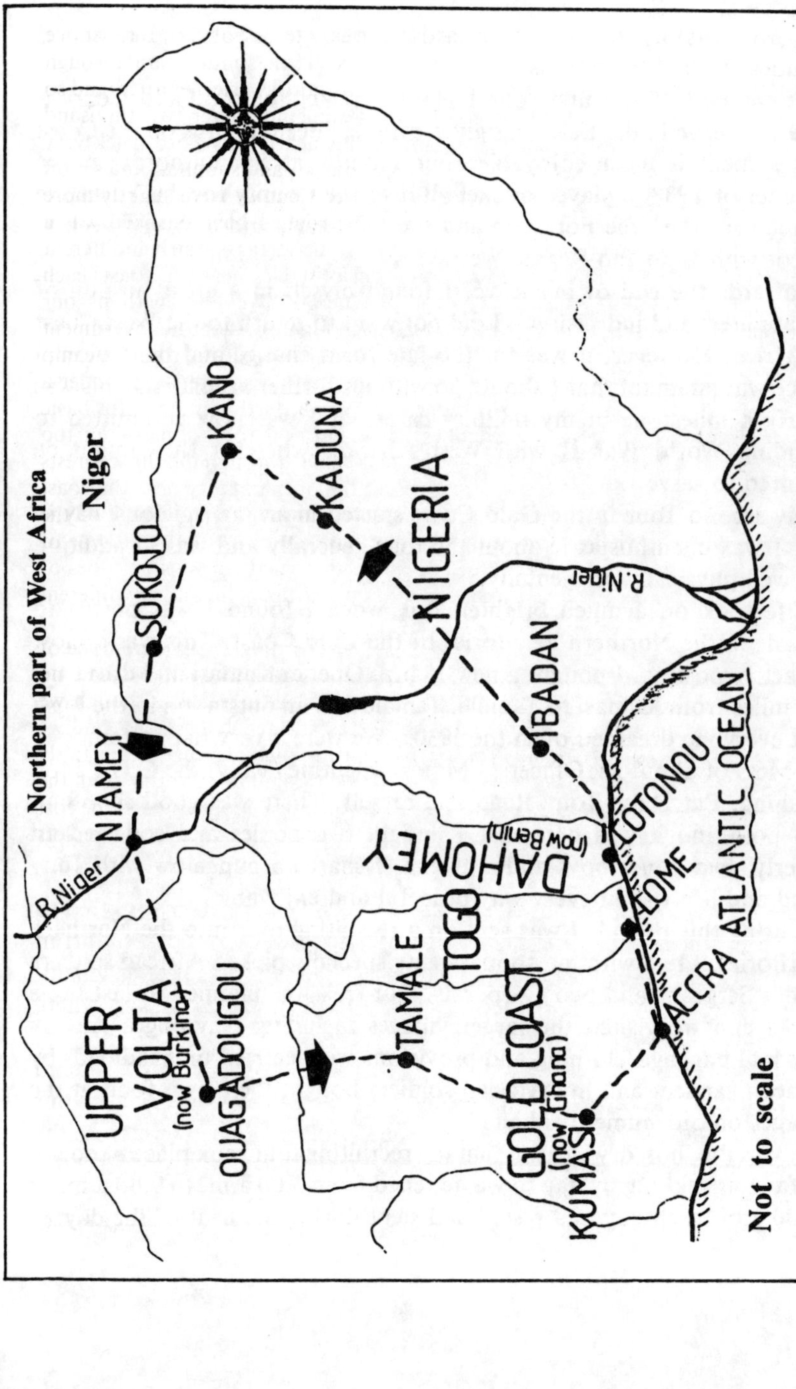

Safari route taken by Lieutenants Read, van Straubenzee, and Boggis, 1937 – approximately 2,000 miles in three weeks.

was Mr. Taylor) steering a hazardous passage across the ravine is included in the illustrations.

At the end of my first tour I played cricket for the Gold Coast *v.* Nigeria. Leave in the U.K. was given after eighteen months on the Coast and I spent a most enjoyable four months at Spennithorne in the Summer of 1938. I played cricket all over the County for the Yorkshire Gentlemen, the Free Foresters and the I Zingari, and a lovely week at Alscot with Izzie and Reggie West.

Towards the end of my leave, I found myself in a great turmoil of unhappiness and indecision - I did not want to return to the West Coast of Africa. However, it was far too late for a change and the Colonial Office was adamant that I should go without further argument. This was clearly a milestone in my military career as I was now committed to spending World War II with West Africans wherever they might be required to serve.

My second Tour in the Gold Coast started in an inauspicious way in that I was unenthusiastic about the tour generally and was in addition not well physically or mentally.

Life took on a much brighter look when I found I was posted to Tamale in the Northern Territories of the Gold Coast. This was a most attractive posting. I bought a new 15 h.p. Opel in Kumasi and drove the 250 miles from Kumasi to Tamale. Tamale was an outstation in the Bush that everyone dreamed of in the 1930s. We were a very happy family in the Mess of about six Officers - Major Valentine (Vally) the C.O., John Leishing, Pat Daly, Tony Read and myself. There was good shooting, and polo and it was here that I bought two ponies and collected an orderly, two house boys and a groom. I shared a bungalow with Tony Read and life was in every way peaceful and enjoyable.

During this period, I was sent on a recruiting tour into the Northern Territories. I had with me about twenty specially picked African soldiers with a Sergeant and two Corporals. Our trek was planned to last three weeks and we visited the larger villages including Navrongo. All my personal baggage/clothing and provisions were carried on headloads by African carriers and my African soldiers bought their own food at the villages on our numerous halts.

It was the 'hot/dry' season that my recruiting tour took place - too hot by far for trekking by day so we marched from 3.00 a.m. to 9.00 a.m. or 10.00 a.m. each day and rested and slept during the heat of the day.

I returned to Tamale with ten new recruits which I believe was considered satisfactory.

Hardly had I recovered from my recruiting tour when I was ordered back to the Northern Territories, this time to patrol crossing places on the River Volta. There was a yellow fever scare and with two platoons my job was to stop any population movements from the North of the Country.

This was a very enjoyable three weeks and I was accompanied by Regimental Sergeant Major McCabe. We used to patrol the Volta River daily visiting the African Section Posts and always took shot guns with us to shoot wild guinea fowl and teal for the pot.

Our African soldiers constructed the local round huts for myself and R.S.M. McCabe and we lived in comparative comfort.

My recollection is that this nomadic life on the Volta River lasted about a month and I cannot say truthfully that we achieved the objects originally planned.

A further brief spell followed in Tamale, polo and a wonderful few days wildfowl shooting in Navrongo with John Lieshing afterwards.

I have not yet mentioned social life on the West Coast in the 1930s. On the Elder Dempster boats in those days there was very heavy drinking, in fact it was said that in one of the wartime voyages when the M.V. *Accra* was torpedoed the old timers in the dining saloon at the time refused to leave their lunch and were consequently lost at sea when the ship foundered.

On the Coast, as I remember we took an enormous amount of exercise, either golf, cricket or polo and evening consumption of alcohol was considerable - half a bottle of gin or whisky per person was not considered excessive, but whisky was occasionally consumed at breakfast from a teapot as camouflage to deceive higher authority.

Sunday lunches of groundnut stew preceded by an enormous amount of gin was a regular weekly entertainment lasting generally to teatime and almost always we retired to bed afterwards.

It was now late 1939 and I remember that we were recalled from that shooting holiday as World War II was upon us and life was to alter in a momentous way.

Mobilization plans for the Gold Coast Regiment was for it to expand to form a Brigade Group of three Battalions, a gunner battery and various odds and sods.

I was selected as Adjutant of 3 Gold Coast Regiment (G.C.R.) and together with Major Frank Clifton (Royal Fusiliers), my first Commanding Officer, had the task of recruiting a thousand totally untrained Africans and training them for War. In this formidable task we were provided with Non-Commissioned Officers (N.C.O.s) and Trained Soldier drafts from the First and Second Battalions to give us (a new Battalion) a framework on which to train our recruits. These days were interesting and very rewarding, it was also encouraging that vast numbers of men came forward prepared to serve anywhere for the duration of the War.

The Battalion's location for its formation was at a diamond mine, Akwatia, near Accra, where the authorities cooperated in giving us the necessary buildings as diamond mining had ceased for the duration.

When the Battalion reached its full establishment in numbers we moved to Winneba, a village on the Sea Coast as the area was excellent for the very strenuous training programme we were about to begin.

It was here that Lieutenant Colonel Tank Western took over command of the Battalion and here it was that our shortages in British Officers and British N.C.O.s were made good from Rhodesia. This requires some explanation as Rhodesia (now Zimbabwe) was at that time a Crown Colony and its mobilization plan was to send drafts of Officers and N.C.O.s to all the West African Colonial Forces to bring them up to War Establishment.

The Rhodesians were a splendid contingent who had left their homes, jobs and families to support the War effort and they soon fitted into the way of things.

I recall Major Noel Reid who became Second-in-Command to Colonel Tank Western, A. D. Campbell Commanding D Company, who was killed at Waddara, and Major Jack French Commanding A Company, and many others, all of whom became great friends.

The Africans built grass huts for both the Officers and themselves at Winneba and I recall a very intensive training programme devised by Colonel Tank Western who was determined that 3 Gold Coast Regiment should be made ready for war in as short a time as possible.

Chapter 3

The Opening of the East African Campaign, 1940–1941

I had been on the coast for nearly two years and despite wartime restrictions I was allowed to go on leave to the U.K. It was early 1940 and the phoney War was on and my passage home in an Elder Dempster boat was uneventful.

I have only hazy recollections of my leave at Spennithorne, rationing, very little petrol and on the whole a very quiet holiday.

My brother, Henry, was serving in the British Expeditionary Force as a G III in the 4th Division and my mother and I were concerned to hear on the news in early May 1940 that the balloon had gone up in Europe and that the British Expeditionary Force were in full retreat.

I had prepared my mother for heavy tidings and when, a few days later, Henry telephoned to say he was safe and on his way home we were overjoyed.

I well remember those marvellous Summer days after Dunkirk when Henry was at home for a few days and we played village cricket at Spennithorne and it was hard to realize that a war was on at all.

Looking back, I recall what my feelings were at that time and being a regular soldier I was anxious to see service somewhere in the world, but I knew that almost certainly it would be with Africans and probably somewhere in Africa.

I remember that this was a somewhat sombre and unsettled wartime leave with little opportunity for enjoyment. I recall receiving a Warning Order from the Colonial Office to be prepared for embarkation (destination unknown) in the near future, September 1940.

I stayed in London at my Club (The R.A.G.) and when I was told of my date for departure my mother came to London and we stayed at Brown's Hotel for my last night in the U.K.

Italy had by then declared war on the British Empire and at the next table to us in Brown's Hotel was the Emperor Haile Selassie of Ethiopia who had been deposed from his Kingdom by the Italians - I was to be one of the first representatives of the East African force to enter Addis Ababa and to put the Lion of Judah back on his throne, but more about this later.

My departure order was to proceed to Southampton and embark on the P. & O. boat *Narkunda* and it was only when I got on board this ship did I know that I was bound for East Africa and probably for war (I had sealed Orders).

The *Narkunda* was one of P. & O.'s old passenger liners and I was soon to find out that my shipmates included fifteen or twenty Officers of the Royal West African Frontier Force also returning from leave to join their Battalion in East Africa.

I was delighted to find that I was to share a cabin with Fergus Higgins, a brother Officer with me in the 43rd and a close friend.

The bulk of the other passengers on the *Narkunda* were Civil Servants returning to their posts in the Far East and many women and children also on return to their head of family from a sojourn in the U.K.

It was, as I remember, only a few weeks after the British Expeditionary Force's evacuation from the beaches of Dunkirk and my thoughts and feelings on leaving England, my family and friends, was one of considerable apprehension.

The *Narkunda* was very much a peacetime passenger liner and as far as I can remember there were a few light aircraft guns distributed on the top deck and we British Officers were required to act as 'look-outs' for submarines at specified times during the day.

There were strict 'blackout' regulations and we had frequent 'life boat' drill.

Apart from these Wartime restrictions life on board was extremely pleasant and there were lashings of food and drink - a splendid orchestra and dancing every night.

It was on this Wartime voyage at an age of 27 that I first fell in love.

Peggy Wilson was 18 and with her mother was on her way to join her father in Singapore. I had never been remotely interested in any girl before and, I suppose, because of this Peggy was to me most attractive, exciting and disturbing and sadly for both of us it resulted in great unhappiness many years later.

These were early days of the War and the convoy system had not got under way and my recollection is that the *Narkunda* sailed entirely alone and relied on her speed to defeat the U-boats. We reached Cape Town in about a month and we received enormous hospitality and welcome from the British South Africans and for two or three days we were entertained most lavishly.

I remember most vividly that two days in Cape Town. I took Peggy to dine at the Mount Nelson Hotel and afterwards to see the film *North West Passage* – I had no thoughts of the War – I was very happy.

In another fortnight we had reached Mombasa and emotional goodbyes with Peggy to whom I had become extremely attached – I wanted to become engaged to her but she said 'No', which was probably a wise decision in view of future events. We agreed to write which in fact we did for many months.

Disembarking at Mombasa, I was pushed into an uncomfortable Transit Camp to await my move to the Northern Frontier District of Kenya where the Gold Coast Brigade was at present in camp.

My experience of Transit Camps in Africa was frustrating and intensely boring and this first occasion was true to form – it was weeks before lorry transport was available to take me, and the journey on indifferent roads and then practically no road, just sand, took about a fortnight.

The weather was very hot by day and lorry transport was uncomfortable and very dusty. The nights on this journey were wonderfully cool and the lorry convoy stopped at about 6.00 p.m. and we had an evening meal mostly out of tins. We slept in our valises under the stars. From Nanuki in Central Kenya the road to the Northern Frontier District became very bad, in fact practically non-existent and we reached our destination, Wajir Fort, after about five days' uncomfortable travel.

I was happy to be with my Battalion again and amongst my friends but it was a pretty soul-destroying time for the Gold Coast Brigade.

Our Battalion position was around Wajir which consisted only of a white fort in the style of Beau Geste – it was very beautiful in the moonlight!!

Life in the Kenya desert was deadly boring and the only event to look forward to was the monthly arrival of mail and our fortnightly ration of one bottle of whisky and a few bottles of beer.

The water was foul – it had a bitter taste and many of us suffered from what we vulgarly called 'Wajir clap' undoubtedly caused from drinking it.

I had resumed my appointment as Adjutant of the Battalion and my job was mainly to draft the orders for the many long-distance patrols sent out to try and find out the whereabouts and disposition of the Italian Forces and Banda in the Buna area.

I remember vividly a big raid on Buna carried out by the whole Battalion all transported in lorries and cars. The distance from Wajir was about seventy miles – all went well to start with but heavy firing from the Italian position in Buna caused the Commanding Officer to call off the attack and return to Wajir.

This first action and the first time we had been under fire was NOT a great success and the Brigadier (Piggy Richards) was not best pleased with us. With hindsight and our later knowledge of the fighting capabilities of the Italians we should have pressed on in a more aggressive way, but this was an experience and we were learning the hard way.

In those early rather boring months I recall my first-ever flight in an aircraft.

It was a two-seater Recce aircraft – a Hartebeest piloted by a mad South African. We were to carry out a reconnaissance of the Italian positions at El Wak about 150 miles from Wajir. This fellow was determined to give me some excitement and he instructed me to man the Bren Gun in the rear of the plane and in addition he did some quite frightening aerobatics including looping the loop. By then I was past caring and was frightfully sick all over his bloody plane. We were fired on by Italian ack-ack at El Wak but I didn't care and on return took to my bed for two days to recover.

The Kenya desert around Wajir was flat, arid and covered with thorn bushes. It was intensely hot by day but pleasantly cool at night – we slept on camp beds with mosquito nets with only the stars above us. The Gold Coast Brigade was encamped around the fort which appeared very romantic in the moonlight – giraffes were the only wild animals we ever saw.

It was after about three months in this godforsaken Northern Frontier District that I and a good friend, Pat Daly, who was a Company Commander in the Battalion, were given three weeks' leave – I was lucky enough to have a cousin Audrey Clark who, with her husband Tom, were farming near Nakuru and Pat and I had the most wonderful holiday.

Everything of the best was given to us by the Settlers and after a riotous week at the Norfolk Hotel, Nairobi, we were back to Wajir in most tedious and uncomfortable lorry transport.

During these months in Wajir I hadn't forgotten Peggy and we wrote to one another fairly frequently and we remained very fond of each other.

By Christmas 1940, I had been in Wajir for some six months and during this time, as I subsequently found, East Africa Command, and in particular my Division (12th African), were making plans for the liberation of Eritrea, Somaliland and Abyssinia.

The Brigadier attached great importance to intensive training in convoy drill, driving with sidelights only at night, and strict distances between vehicles.

Motor transport consisted of saloon cars for the Officers and open lorries for the Africans, the troops always sitting facing outwards and ready to dismount speedily on threat of enemy action.

El Wak

The period of stalemate in the East African campaign came to an end with the raid on El Wak. In this raid the whole Gold Coast Brigade took part supported by a Battalion of South African troops and South African tanks and the East African Recce Squadron (Armoured Cars).

It was indeed an enormous convoy of lorries and carriers and we travelled an immense distance entirely by night and totally unsuspected by the Italians.

We flung ourselves in overwhelming strength upon the Italian fort at El Wak.

That the operation was entirely successful was not surprising as it was one of the few occasions in the campaign when our force was in every department superior in numbers and equipment to those of the enemy.

El Wak was important in three ways. Firstly, it was a most useful rehearsal for the subsequent invasion of Somaliland. Secondly, it gave our Gold Coast troops a valuable experience of war with the Italians at almost negligible losses; and thirdly, it did untold damage to Italian morale from which they never recovered.

I remember the task of the 3rd Gold Coast Regiment was the capture of the air field which in fact we took with no opposition at all.

Looking back, I think what stands out to me in this truly spectacular raid was the distance covered (Garissa to El Wak is approximately 250 miles) in complete darkness by some 150–200 vehicles.

The large majority of drivers were African with little experience of night driving and with only side lights. The journey took about eight hours and the whole Brigade column reached the rendezvous just short of El Wak at first light and ready for the assault.

Operational secrecy was complete and total surprise achieved.

It has always been a source of wonderment to me as to how vehicle maintenance was achieved on quite frightful roads, sometimes in intense heat or alternatively in heavy rain and mud. I well remember Lieutenant Peter Hardman, the Battalion Motor Transport Officer with his maintenance lorries always at the rear of the column to deal with breakdowns.

He did a magnificent job.

We had to carry all our petrol in four-gallon petrol cans, many of which leaked.

The initial advance was carried out over the waterless desert land of Kenya and Somaliland so water for both troops and vehicles had to be carried.

These facts are given because the business of the administration of the Gold Coast Brigade in this campaign was a nightmare.

After the Italian defeat at El Wak, General Simone (the Italian General Officer Commanding) found it necessary to issue the following message to all the troops in the area of the Juba:

> 'In some units there is little zest. In some parts of the front, the defensive organization has been carried out with a rudimentary conception that calls to mind the primitive military art of the Negus. This bears witness to the incapacity, the indolence of the men or, even worse, the incapacity of the responsible commander. Training in most cases is not observed; at the most it consists of a few haphazard hours of instruction in the use of Company or Platoon, a little arms drill badly carried out, and a little theoretical teaching in obvious and monotonous subjects. Nobody pays any attention to the war training of Company or Battalion. There are many who know just enough to keep their ranks and that is all. This war which we are at this moment fighting against the English calls for the most sagacious and intelligent application of the latest tactical principles as evolved in the great modern armies and not those of primordial systems of guerilla warfare against Abyssinian rebels, unled and like hunted gazelles.'

We had now been in Kenya for six months and Christmas 1940 was spent in a rest area near Nairobi. In the New Year we moved to the Tana River near Garissa where we carried out specialized training in river crossings.

I well remember an occasion when the Commanding Officer and I (Adjutant) visited two Companies at work on the river - ostensibly a rehearsal for a possible opposed river crossing in the future. It was a wonderfully cheering sight - about 500 African soldiers really enjoying themselves splashing about in the warm water. The Commanding Officer (Tank Western) wasn't too pleased but I said, 'Let them play, they haven't had fun like this for six months', and so the water 'jamboree' continued and some serious training was carried out.

During the last months of 1940 and in the New Year of 1941 East African command had finalized plans for the conquest of Italian Somaliland and Abyssinia and to put back Haile Selassie (The Lion of Judah) on his throne.

The East African Campaign (1940–1941)

It would seem to me essential at this stage to give a brief outline of the East African Campaign, the Force involved and the vast area covered in the forthcoming operations.

The general object of the Campaign was the total defeat and destruction of the Italian forces South of Addis Ababa including the Lakes and the Force consisted only of the 11th and 12th African Divisions under the command of Lieutenant General Sir Alan Cunningham.

12th African Division to which I belonged as Adjutant of 3rd Gold Coast Regiment in 24 Gold Coast Brigade was to advance North from Wajir in the Northern Frontier District in Kenya whilst the 11th African Division was to move South from Addis Ababa, thereby hopefully producing a pincer movement designed to squeeze and destroy the complete Italian Army within the area mentioned above.

The forthcoming story explains how this was done and my involvement in it as Adjutant of 3rd Gold Coast Regiment.

The map on p. 39 will help the reader to follow the story.

On February 9th, 1941, the great advance for which we had waited so long began, with the whole Gold Coast Brigade involved.

By this time our training for war had reached a high standard of efficiency, our motor convoy drill was excellent. We had captured Afmadu by the end of the month and after 2 Gold Coast Regiment's resounding success in its first battle at Burro Errillo we were poised to cross the Juba River on February 20th. The crossing was in fact unopposed and the River was so low that we were able to walk across it.

Enormous and complicated arrangements had been taken to provide assault boats and taping of the route to the River, none of which were required.

A few days later we moved on very fast, attacking and capturing the town of Gelib in Somaliland and taking a huge number of prisoners, war material, and stores including Italian wines.

After Gelib we moved to an area North-West of the town to mop up and restore order over a wide section of Somaliland.

Those were busy days for a Regimental Adjutant and 3 Gold Coast Regiment and its Companies covered a huge area and administration was a nightmare.

Despite this extremely active and exciting life, I still found time to write to Peggy and though mail was painfully slow both ways I was able to keep in touch with her and she with me and I believe we were still in love with one another.

During this period of active patrolling we captured the remnants of the Italian 100th Division including an Italian Brigade Commander and many Italian Officers, after which peace and order were more or less restored.

We found the majority of Italian Officers extraordinarily nice people whose heart was not in the War. They gave no trouble as prisoners of war and in fact wished to remain as close to us as possible for fear of being slaughtered by the 'Shifta'.

The 'Shifta' as their name implies were happy to liquidate any nationality, British or Italian, for personal gain of loot from the British and revenge in the case of the Italians.

As a change from fighting, during the next few weeks the Gold Coast Brigade took over the administration of the Juba area and my Battalion was given sectors of responsibility.

With the help of Italian officials who had been left behind we covered an area up to Iscaia Baidowa and Lugh Ferrandi and helped to reduce the chaos into which war and the collapse of the Juba defences had thrown the country along the upper reaches of the river.

Everywhere the local inhabitants seemed delighted to see the last of the Italians and the Gold Coast Brigade made friends very quickly.

My Battalion (3rd Gold Coast) now moved to Neghelli with no opposition and it was here that we took over extremely comfortable buildings with large quantities of tinned food and wines left by the Italians.

In the house occupied by Battalion H.Q. we found a refrigerator in excellent working order and we lived in great comfort for about ten days.

This rest was short-lived and soon we were on the move North once again and intelligence had told us of considerable Italian forces located North-West of Neghelli.

It was here that 3 Gold Coast Regiment Battalion H.Q. intercepted an Italian wireless message for higher authority which read, 'I hear the sound of many truck engines, attack by an armoured regiment imminent'. This indicates the poor state of enemy intelligence and the state of the Italian nerves – we actually only had six Carden Lloyd Bren Carriers!!

Intensive reconnaissance and probing of the enemy positions was now the order of the day and one of our literary geniuses wrote the following light-hearted description of a reconnaissance in force in preparation for heavy fighting in the days ahead.

Cow Gun Corner

During the week before we crossed the river Juba, the Powers That Be took it into their heads, for some unknown reason, to organize the daily excursions to visit Cow Gun Corner, a charming little spot nestling on the banks of the tropical river.

The excursion always left about the same time, and every day one met the same crowd waiting on the transport, each man with a ration of lunch in his haversack and looking forward to a good day's sport. On this particular expedition which proved to be the last of an exciting series, it was decided to send a strong force commanded by the Battalion Second-in-Command, Major Noel Reid. Major Reid was a colourful character and very popular with all ranks in the Battalion. His enthusiasm for offensive action was legendary, hence his battle cry of 'Oke and Jake', 'Let's go' appears many times in the frivolous description of this day by one of the many young Officers taking part.

Major Reid had Captain van Straubenzee as his Adjutant, two Rifle Companies under the command of Major Jack French and Captain Rex Ames and two 3″ Mortar Sections commanded by Messrs Merlin and Thompson. In addition, we had the support of the Gold Coast Regiment Light Battery and the East African Reconnaissance Squadron of armoured cars (the Rekkies) altogether a formidable mixed force.

And so, off we went – only half an hour late; 'the timing is obviously going to play an important part in today's drive through the coverts', said somebody. On the way we accumulated a troop of armoured cars and the light battery and having duly reached the recognized parking place we got off and as usual hung about waiting for something to happen while the gunners scattered their pieces about.

In case you were one of the unfortunate who did not make the trip, there follows a brief description of Cow Gun Corner – the Jewel of Somaliland. A narrow road runs up to the Corner, with the bush, thin at first, getting thicker and more prickly as you proceed until it becomes a dense wall of spines on either side at a stretch known as Euphorbia Avenue. At one place on the way up there is a small clearing where the enemy, entering into the spirit of the game, very sportingly put up an ambush for us on a previous occasion. And so on to the little twist in the road called Cow Gun Corner – if you still wanted to go further (God help you if you did!) you came to a big clearing covered with a lot of long grass and a bit of barbed wire. On the far side, in the inviting shade of some fine trees was a village of grass huts – the 'Haunt of The Wily Wop'.

But, to get back to the story, while we waited by the lorries Major French, who was to attempt to cut through the bush and outflank the enemies left, was sent off on his heart-breaking task with the usual hearty 'Right! off you go'.

Having given Major French a bit of a start there was a fresh outburst of Oking and Jaking and the rest of us streamed off up the road.

On each previous trip our arrival had been signalled to the Wops further up by a couple of signal bombs in the bush and sure enough, we hadn't gone four hundred yards when – 'Bang-Bang' – the bombs went off and the game was on. Once we paused while Bomber pooped off with his mortars, 'just to stir 'em up a bit' as he said, and during this performance while the others tried to find a bit of shade, there was a rustling in the bush followed by the appearance of two stalwart troops dragging with them a very old and decrepit Somali. 'E day for bush Sah' they said and with no further ado the old boy was accused of having let off the signal bombs and carefully guarded.

The rest of the trip was uneventful – we approached The Corner with great stealth but not a sound broke the torrid silence. All previous excursionists had been greeted at this point with bursts of machine gun fire, rifles, grenades, and even the 'Cow Gun', which received its name at this very corner, had whistled over the trees. But today we got right up to the open space and selected positions for the various parts of our force and there was never a sound.

My mortar was set up behind an ant hill on the edge of the clearing while Bomber found a convenient hollow from which to carry on his pet hobby, and behind us under a big tree Major Reid, Philip and the Battery Commander accompanied by an 18 set established their H.Q.

'Oke and Jake?' I *knew* who *that* was. 'Plaster those trees and huts with a few bombs.' So the mortars set to work and soon the dust was rising and the huts tottering. Oking and Jaking was also going on in H.Q. where the signaller was announcing loudly and without any result that Noel was calling Jack. Unfortunately Jack was unable to call Noel which made if difficult and so the signaller went on with his loud and mournful dirge.

Soon the Major reappeared, this time silhouetted against the sky, standing on an ant hill. He was showing the familiar and dangerous symptoms: head thrown back, lips drawn tight and looking most aggressive. 'Nobody here!' he snorted. 'Oke and Jake we'll advance.' Our hearts fell – that open space with the wire looked so utterly bare of cover. To his everlasting glory, Jeffries, one of the forward Pl. Commanders, at this moment let off a round which was instantly greeted by heavy machine gun, rifle, and Cow Gun fire from all sides. The Major hurriedly left his pedestal on the ant hill and looked less aggressive as he took cover from the bullets which were whipping the dust off the top of his ant hill. 'Thank God,' we all thought, 'the situation is temporarily saved even if we can't advance.'

But our thankful prayers were soon cut short – the Major had another idea. 'Hear that machine gun over there?' he asked, pointing at the blank wall of bush three yards away. 'Oke and Jake give it three bombs.' I gave it three bombs and it stopped for a few moments, meanwhile Bomber was loosing off from his retreat in the hollow and the Major dashed back to H.Q. to ask for news of Major French's progress only to hear that he was still miles away and hacking his way painfully through thick bush. Philip was sending back latest reports of the engagement to Battalion H.Q. – the Armoured Cars were out in the clearing blazing away and the Battery Commander had his guns going. It was hell, man.

The delay in the flank attack was having an obvious effect on the Major and when I arrived at H.Q. he and Philip van Straubenzee were taking it in turns to climb up the big tree to try and see something. Neither could see anything, and Philip remembering something about discretion and valour was suggesting that it was about time to send another message instead of going up that tree again (these Wops *do* shoot so high).

No hope of Major French arriving for ages – 'Oke and Jake,' cried the Major, 'Christ' we thought 'Now what?' 'Only one thing for it,' he whipped out, 'dig in for the night' (it was 1330 hours!). 'But we've no mortar ammunition left' – 'Oke and Jake – Armoured Cars – off you go – get the reserve mortar ammunition.'

We went back to our mortars feeling rather despondent – in this bush the Wop would be able to creep up to within five yards of us without being seen. Anyway we had to cross the road with a heavy machine gun firing down it.

Firing went on madly till some time after 4.00 p.m. when Major French came in behind us to everybody's unbounded relief. 'We won't have to dig in for the night now,' we thought; and we were right, thank heaven.

The Major, looking somewhat disappointed, ordered us to withdraw. So we trooped slowly back to the lorries with Major Reid muttering at frequent intervals, 'It's a bastard', with obvious feeling.

But it had been a good if at times alarming day with all those disturbing 'Oke and Jake we'll advance – or dig in for the night', they certainly kept the pace and excitement going.

'Everyone on the lorries?' 'Ready to go?' 'Oke and Jake – off you go.'

This particular patrol had a sad ending as Major Disney Roebuck, the Commander of the Gold Coast Battery, received a bullet in his stomach – we wanted to evacuate him but he wouldn't leave the Battery.

At the end of the day there was no other answer but for the Battalion Medical Officer, Joe Innes, to carry out a major operation to extract the bullet.

This must have been one of the strangest of all settings for hazardous surgery – a dilapidated shed with a leaking roof, and a rickety wooden table on which to work. Taking part were Joe Innes, with only the barest selection of surgical instruments required, the Commanding Officer Tank Western to administer the anaesthetic and myself, the Adjutant, to hold a hurricane lamp, no other light was available. We were able to extract the bullet but I remember that it was a bitterly cold and wet night and despite wrapping poor Disney up in many blankets we could not keep him warm. He died the next day of shock and exposure – he was a most gallant Officer and a great loss to the Gold Coast Brigade.

So by May 2nd, after about a fortnight's patrolling by day and night in the unpleasant conditions already described, we had forced the Italians to relinquish their forward positions and now knew the extent of their main defences at Waddara.

Whilst these operations were going on a tragic accident happened in 3 Gold Coast Regiment – in their headlong flight, the Italians had left a pile of hand grenades (red letter box bombs, we used to call them). A number of our British N.C.O.s including a Company Sergeant Major were practising throwing these lethal weapons and one was dropped in error setting off the whole heap.

The carnage was indescribably horrific and a number of our British N.C.O.s lost arms and legs – I will never forget this incident and, as Adjutant, I assisted the Battalion Medical Officer, Joe Innes, to administer morphine – no-one survived.

I think it was during this period that I began to forget Peggy Wilson and in any event though the mail became less and less I had not received any letter from her for many weeks and there the matter stood for the foreseeable future.

Chapter 4

The Battle of Waddara

In writing the story of this Great Battle, I have relied heavily on the despatches of the War Correspondent of the *East African Standard*, the late George Kinnear, together with the official account of the operation by the late Brigadier C.E.M. Richards, C.B.E., D.S.O., M.C., who was commanding the Gold Coast Brigade.

Opposed to the Gold Coast Brigade was a complete Italian Division occupying a very strong natural position; and due to the persistent probing tactics of our patrols, the enemy abandoned their outpost positions and withdrew to their main defensive stronghold around Waddara which lies thirty miles North of Neghelli.

Waddara is a name which figures prominently in Abyssinian history. It was there that in 1935 Ras Desta held up an Italian force for nearly twelve months when Neghelli changed hands three times in desperate fighting. Italian aircraft bombed the gallant Ethiopians in this town but always Ras Desta's troops withdrew to Waddara, a stronghold where they were able to resist enemy onslaughts for a long time.

The Italians knew Waddara well and confidently felt that they could hold and defeat any attacking force.

The road North from Neghelli runs across a great and steep valley, and, on the slopes and ridges beyond, the enemy had converted the natural features into a stronghold of immense strength on a narrow front of a few miles. On their right were mountains offering commanding positions for their guns which could with ease dominate the valley and sweep the main road south of it. In the middle was Waddara and on the enemy's left was the worst of all features from our point of view, a dense African forest, an obstacle that is rare in Abyssinian warfare. There is no doubt of the tremendous advantage a forest gives to a defending force. It is practically invisible, its strength unknown, its movements uncertain and it offers no information or target from the air.

Mechanized forces cannot operate in it and its undergrowth and open spaces are alike full of traps for an attacking force. It was mainly in this great forest that the battle of Waddara was bitterly fought and won. Grass slopes fell gently to the lip of the valley, which in places was a stark gorge 100 feet deep. The Italians had built their defences several miles deep, cut tunnels in the hills and hidden their artillery and their maze of machine gun posts with unusual ability. The whole area was a vast tangle of hills, forest and ravines held by four battalions of Italian troops with more battalions in reserve.

When the Gold Coast came up against this apparently impregnable stronghold the first forward battalion was rested while the others took a hand. Our force consisted of the Gold Coast Brigade of three battalions, Gold Coast artillery, an East African machine gun company, and a squadron of East African armoured cars, our old acquaintances the Rekkies. Later, light South African artillery was added for the final assault. For a fortnight, from the third week in April to May 2nd, our force probed the position. The enemy had eventually to be turned out of it and the problem was how to do it with the minimum of loss.

So for that fortnight the Italians were harassed relentlessly. Day and night our patrols went out doing the difficult and dangerous but necessary job of finding out and fixing the enemy posts. Coloured Very lights shattered the darkness of the night as the patrols worked the country systematically and kept the enemy's nerves on edge. Captured Italian bombs were hurled into the ravine, echoing with appalling crashes, to add noise to the nerve-wracking siege. Every kind of ingenious devilment that could be thought of was tried to destroy Italian morale and confuse the position. Even the baboons were our allies! They careered about the hillsides at night and drew bursts of machine-gun and rifle fire from the Italians who were becoming increasingly fearful.

There was no need for the enemy to be so nervous for they had great superiority in numbers. General Pralormo had in the Waddara area the 24th Division of six battalions, reinforced by Blackshirts Battalions, and at least twenty-two guns. Most of his Colonial Infantry were strengthened by hard-fighting Eritreans and he had all the advantages of a chosen and well-developed position. The Gold Coast troops displayed great courage and daring during that initial fortnight.

The Battle was divided into three phases, the first being the assault and capture of the enemy forward positions (April 19th to April 22nd), the second a period of patrolling and fixing enemy positions (April 23rd to May 2nd), and the third the attack and capture of the enemy main position (May 3rd to May 10th).

3 G.C.R. (Gold Coast Regiment), the Battalion about which my story is mainly concerned, was given the tasks indicated in Phases I and II and we had with us and under command, a Light Battery Royal Artillery, a squadron of armoured cars and two platoons of irregulars. During this period we carried out a series of successful attacks on the enemy forward positions and by April 21st he had withdrawn to his main position, a distance of two miles. The armoured cars and irregulars combined most effectively with the Battalion, capturing much enemy material, including machine guns and many prisoners. Very heavy losses were inflicted on the Italian forces.

Though I myself, as Adjutant of 3 G.C.R., did not take part in the patrolling except for the occasion already mentioned (Cow Gun Corner) I used to visit the Rifle Companies daily and this was a most hazardous mission because the journeys were sometimes through enemy country where snipers lurked and enemy patrols were often very active.

I learnt a lot from those visits to the companies and was able to get first-hand knowledge from the patrol commanders themselves of the really unpleasant conditions under which they were operating.

Rum was in short supply and there were no comforts for these troops on their return to their companies, usually late at night or in the early dawn, and it was remarkable that, however wet and cold they were, their morale and spirits remained high.

In Phase II we continued with active patrolling both by day and night but on a larger scale. The Italian main defences were formidable and very cleverly sited in a naturally strong position. On the enemy right were high features culminating in the centre into two peaks christened by us as the Twin Pimples. The ground then fell away into thick impenetrable forest intersected with various small open glades. In front and parallel to the position ran a very deep ravine nearly 100 feet in depth and full of very thick undergrowth. From this ravine ran many branch ravines of varying depth and the whole country was one great tangle, most deceptive to observe and most difficult for our companies in which to operate.

We soon found the enemy's defences on the right flank, they were firmly established on some high ground, and Ethiopian Patriots, experts in bushcraft, helped us in this vital task. The ground to the North of this feature fell away to a precipice and several actions were fought in this area, heavy casualties inflicted on the enemy and two machine guns captured.

The Italian left proved most difficult to break, as it was situated in very thick forest country. Deserters gave us wrong information and finally it was our own patrols working chiefly by night who gave us the vital intelligence which was that the enemy's left flank terminated in an open glade some 3,000 yards from the Twin Pimples. These patrols were carried out under terrible conditions, often in torrential rain and through vile country and the young British Officers, British N.C.O.s and their Africans taking part in these operations were totally exhausted at the end of this fortnight. My recollection is that whether we were out on operations or not the nights were bitterly cold and we did not have sufficient blankets.

Enemy deserters came in at the rate of about forty a day – and they all told the same story of poor food, no sleep and a general condition of exhausted men fed up with war. A deserter is usually a source of information, but his story has to be fully tested before reliance can be placed upon it and the Intelligence Officers were busy day and night piecing together the tales they were told and fitting them into the picture which, by now, was nearing completion.

Finally, from prisoners and deserters it was determined that the Italian 24th Division commanded by General the Count Pralormo was defending the Waddara position, their front from left to right by the following Italian Units and attached troops – 183 Battalion, 185 Battalion, 7 Battalion, and 54 Battalion, and with 200 Blackshirts in reserve. These troops organized into two Brigades the 25th and 85th. They had twelve guns and some mortars.

During the first two phases we had a number of casualties both European and African and Captain A. D. Campbell commanding D Company 3 G.C.R. was killed when gallantly leading his company in an attack on Waddara House. A. D. was a Rhodesian schoolmaster and a most charming man, respected and liked by both Officers and Africans in 3 G.C.R. There were many courageous acts during that fortnight of overwork and strain and a young Officer, whilst leading his platoon during an attack on a machine gun post, was shot while in the act of hurling a grenade. As he lay dying he told another officer who was with him to take the grenade from his hand before it exploded to kill others. He died, but owing to heavy enemy fire it was impossible to bring him in. Later a patrol collected his body and he was buried with full military honours.

By May 2nd, 3 G.C.R. had done its job, we knew the full extent of Italian positions but we knew also that the assault on Waddara would be no easy task. In this type of country, broken, mountainous, ill supplied with roads, with a dense forest to contend with and an enemy force three times the size of ours meant that considerable risks were to be taken.

On May 1st, the Gold Coast Brigade was ordered to attack and capture the Waddara position and the force available was:

1 G.C.R.
2 G.C.R.
3 G.C.R.
'A' Squadron Armed Cars.
51 G.C. Light Battery.
7 Field Battery South African Forces.
52 Field Company Royal Engineers.
'A' Company (Machine Gun) 1/3 King's African Rifles.
Three platoons of irregular patriots.

The plan was for 2 G.C.R. (the Battalion whose adjutant was Tony Read) and two platoons of irregulars to make a long approach march by day, climb the rock escarpment and attack the Italian left flank in the forest the following day. 1 G.C.R. were to send two companies to move up towards the Pimples but not to become heavily engaged in this very strongly held area. Remaining companies of 1 G.C.R. and irregulars were to demonstrate against the enemy right flank without becoming heavily engaged.

My Battalion 3 G.C.R. were to be ready to advance should the enemy front collapse and a Troop of armoured cars was to endeavour to work forward into the bush on the enemy left when the attack by 2 G.C.R. started to develop. An elaborate artillery programme was worked out to start in the early hours of May 4th.

The whole plan was designed to sweep up the Italian left forward position and the objective given was the main road from Waddara house to a point on the road 600 yards North-West. It was considered that by rolling up the enemy left, he would be forced to evacuate his strong position on the right. Owing to the tangled and complicated country over which 2 G.C.R. had to march, the administrative problem was a nightmare. No motor transport could be used and there was no pack transport available; evacuation of casualties if the attack failed was a major consideration but if successful it might be possible to use an old Abyssinian track of which we knew.

At 0700 hours on May 3rd, 2 G.C.R. began their flanking march which was carried out with utmost precision. By 1730 hours one Company was in position on the escarpment, which had been occupied the previous day by a platoon of irregulars.

The Battalion marched in bare feet, carried two days' rations, one blanket and gas capes. One extra Medical Officer and twenty-four extra stretcher bearers accompanied the force.

On May 4th the battle began. The Artillery, firing on arranged programme, commenced firing at 0545 hours, commencing on the enemy right, then the Pimples and finally on the left.

Coordination of times of Artillery Programme had been difficult to arrange, owing to the uncertainty of the time when the Battalion would make contact.

Two Companies 1 G.C.R., who had crossed the deep ravine during the night May 3rd–4th, began to approach the Pimples about 0730 hours. This move produced very heavy fire. Enemy machine guns and Artillery fired on all the ground in front of Pimples and back areas. Firing also could be heard from our extreme left.

About 0745 hours heavy firing broke out in the Glade area on enemy left, showing that 2 G.C.R. was coming into action. Nothing could be seen of this fighting owing to the thick forest.

One Troop armoured cars were ordered at 0800 hours to move forward to assist attack of 2 G.C.R. They crossed a low ravine over army track which had been put down by the Royal Engineers the night before. Working up the old Abyssinian track, they emerged successfully into the Glade, and engaged five enemy machine gun posts. They inflicted heavy casualties, and had a great moral effect on the exchanged tasks. Unfortunately the new Troop, thinking that the enemy had no artillery weapons, remained in a very confined space in the Glade, firing at the machine gun posts.

The enemy meanwhile had brought up a 65–70 mm gun from the rear, opened fire on the Troop at point blank range, knocked out three Armoured Fighting Vehicles completely destroying two, and killing five of the personnel. One other Armoured Fighting Vehicle was damaged by shell fire at Squadron H.Q. in the back area.

Heavy fighting was still in progress in the Forest, and the right forward Company of 1 G.C.R. on French Hill was ordered to work round and come in on 2 G.C.R. left.

From 1100 hours to 1400 hours, the situation appeared to be developing into stalemate.

Two Companies 1 G.C.R. were pinned to the ground by machine gun fire below the Pimples. 2 G.C.R. seemed to be held in the forest, and the armoured cars had withdrawn slightly. Artillery could not be used to help our Infantry owing to the uncertainty of their positions.

At 1430 hours, news was received that 'A' Company 2 G.C.R. commanded by Captain Maclean had worked through the forest on to the old Abyssinian track, come in on the enemy's left rear and was sweeping all before him. He captured 6 machine guns, 1 mortar, 1 65/77 mm gun and 60 prisoners. Being unable to stop, owing to the progress of the fighting, he disarmed the prisoners and ordered them to our lines. He destroyed the machine guns, removed the breechblock of the gun and the mortar sights. These machine guns and mortar were later retrieved by the enemy and the prisoners never came in.

The dashing attack of Captain Maclean's Company enabled the remaining Companies 2 G.C.R. and one Company 1 G.C.R. to get on.

The enemy could be observed from Battle Headquarters running away from the Waddara House area and Artillery fire was brought down upon them with good effect.

Darkness had now fallen and nothing more could be done that night as the troops were utterly exhausted.

On May 5th the battle continued. Two Companies of 2 G.C.R. and one Company 1 G.C.R. reached their objective and the House Area cleared. The remaining Company 2 G.C.R. under Captain Criddle pushed West across the road and made a very gallant attack on the Pimples. They made very good progress, inflicted heavy casualties on the enemy. They were heavily counter-attacked when near the right Pimple and forced to withdraw suffering some casualties. Patrols were sent out from forward Companies, and the captured positions consolidated. One Company 1 G.C.R. was withdrawn to its original position on French Hill, finally coming back into Brigade reserve.

2 G.C.R. withdrew to the old Abyssinian track with one Company in the Glade and 3 G.C.R. moved forward to house area, and two

Companies 1 G.C.R. were withdrawn from the Pimple area the night of May 5th–6th.

On May 6th 2 G.C.R. and 3 G.C.R. continued active patrolling with a view to continuing the attack on May 7th. In view of their efforts of the three previous days, the perseverance of 2 G.C.R. deserves the highest praise. 3 G.C.R. patrols brought in most valuable information.

Owing to the dense impenetrable forest, in which 2 and 3 G.C.R. were now operating, it was extremely difficult to find the enemy left. He was known to be occupying a feature just East of the road, which it was not possible for Artillery to observe.

On May 7th 3 G.C.R. were to attack this position with two Companies moving on a compass bearing through the Forest, to come in on the rear of the enemy position. 2 G.C.R. were to continue their advance along the old Abyssinian track and attack any position contacted.

Owing to the difficult country and the fact that the Abyssinian track after turning West apparently petered out, the leading Companies of 2 and 3 G.C.R. made contact. The enemy positions were attacked but was unsuccessful, owing to heavy machine gun fire.

It was impossible to use any supporting weapons. Both Battalions were ordered to withdraw to original positions.

On May 9th 2 G.C.R. sent two Companies down the Abyssinian track. Contact was made with the enemy in the same area.

One Company 3 G.C.R. supported by another Company moved up to the Pimples. This feature was occupied by 1015 hours, the enemy having hurriedly evacuated. Two 66–70 mm guns and some material were captured. The position attacked on May 7th was also evacuated by the enemy that evening. The retiring enemy slipped away between two Companies of 2 G.C.R. in a North-East direction at dusk in torrential rain through the thick forest and were unfortunately only observed by a runner.

At 1400 hours on May 9th a Royal Engineers working party, who had gone forward to clear away road obstructions, was heavily fired upon and had to withdraw. This party of the enemy, who attacked the working party, was the same as that seen departing later in the evening.

By the morning of May 10th, the enemy had evacuated the whole of his front- and second-line positions, thus giving up one of the strongest natural positions it is possible to conceive.

At 0600 hours on May 10th, 1 G.C.R. commenced the advance on Adola.

The road was strewn with tree trunks, anti-tank traps, minefields and road demolitions. Progress was slow and no Motor Transport could be used.

At 1630 hours 1 G.C.R. bumped the enemy rear guard approximately nine miles from the Waddara House.

The enemy consisting of Blackshirts and Colonial Infantry with machine guns attacked the flanks, but were driven off with heavy losses, including one Officer killed and one wounded and taken prisoner. The fighting continued throughout the night of May 10th–11th, the enemy finally withdrawing.

Thus ended the Battle of Waddara, the stiffest fight the Brigade had encountered in this War and one which will be long remembered by those who took part in it.

A recently joined British Sergeant-Major who took part in the fighting in Libya stated, 'Bardia was a skirmish, compared with this'.

Every credit is due to the courage and untiring perseverance with which all ranks fought, resulting in the enemy finally collapsing and evacuating his strong position.

Our casualties from April 19th–May 11th were:

	Killed	*Wounded*	*Missing*	*Died of Wounds*
Europeans	13	21	–	1
Africans	31	69	4×	4

Casualties inflicted on the enemy were considerable. It is estimated that 20 Europeans and 150 Africans were killed, and at least four times that number wounded. In addition heavy casualties from our bombing and shelling were reported by deserters. The forest near the Glade area was a charnel house and the stench in the forest for days afterwards was almost unbearable, in spite of the fact that on the night of May 4th–5th the enemy returned to recover what dead they could find.

	DESERTERS	*PRISONERS* EUROPEANS	AFRICANS
Up to May 2nd	133	–	4
May 3rd–11th	128	3	174

WAR MATERIAL CAPTURED OR ABANDONED OR BROUGHT IN BY DESERTERS

3 65/70 mm gun (1 recovered by enemy after we had removed breechblock).

9 heavy machine guns (5 recovered by enemy after we had damaged main parts).

2 Breda Guns.

1 Mortar (recovered by enemy after we removed sights and damaged mortar).

Large number of rifles.
Large quantities amm. of all kinds
1 motor cycle.
Medical stores.
A number of mules.
A quantity of signal equipment.

A number of ponies
A number of donkeys.
A number of cows, etc.
Some saddlery.
Large quantity of equipment.
R.E. tools and electric light set.

THE BATTLE OF WADDARA

Force Commander:- **General the Count Pralormo.**

Italian Forces Involved:-

24th Italian Division. Two Blackshirt Battalions.
Six Infantry Battalions. Twenty Two Guns.

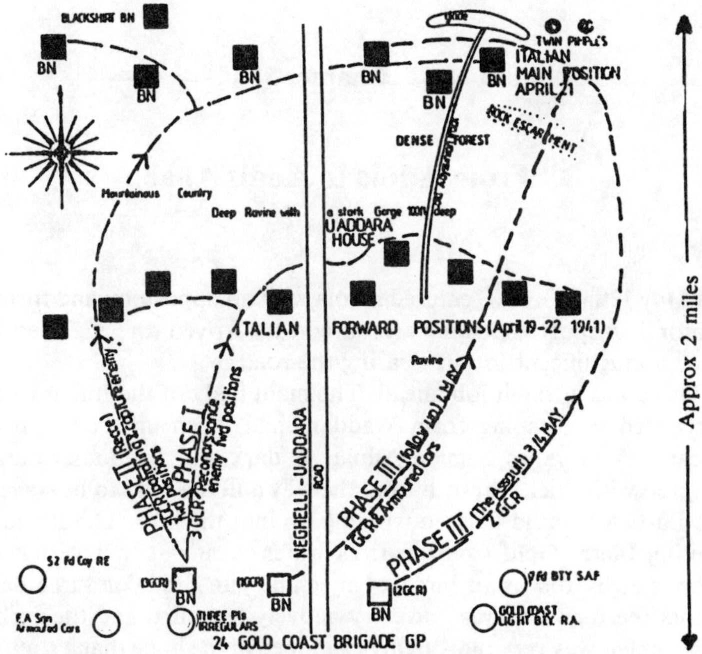

Force Commander:- Brigadier C. E. M. Richards, C.B.E., D.S.O.

British Forces Involved:-

British & South African Force 24th Gold Coast Brigade. R.W.A.F.F.
Three Infantry Battalions of the Gold Coast Regiment.
'A' Squadron East African Armoured Cars.
One Gold Coast Light Battery R.A.
One Field Battery South African Forces.
One Field Company R.E. Gold Coast.
Three Platoons of Irregular Patriots.
One Company (Machine Guns 1/3 Kings African Rifles).

British Forces □

Not to scale

Italian Forces ■

The Battle of Waddara.

Chapter 5

From Adola to Addis Ababa

On May 12th 1 G.C.R. entered Adola with no opposition and fortunately Motor Transport and some armoured cars arrived, the engineers having done a magnificent job in clearing the road.

There was a tough job ahead. The main body of the Italians who had succeeded in escaping from Waddara had taken up their positions at Afrara a few miles outside Adola. A dark and ominous escarpment covered with thick forest, barred the way and the road to be travelled by the Battalion could be seen winding up into the hills. The Italians were waiting there. Gold Coast patrols which went out to investigate were soon met by the usual burst of machine gun fire. For three days and nights the forward area was very actively patrolled and the forbidding escarpment was very thoroughly examined in the hope that a route would be found which would avoid the risk of a frontal advance along a road which the enemy had 'taped'. But there was no alternative. The shaggy forest covering the face of the escarpment was too dense to penetrate and the formation of the wall of mountain-side offered no other way over than the main road.

The Battalion set off from Adola on May 18th and met road conditions of the most discouraging kind, seasoned though they were to rain and mud and foot-slogging and pushing transport through rivers and over rocks. Bridges had been broken down, the roads were mostly under water, a large number of trees had been felled, and wrecked and abandoned Italian lorries of the largest type were used to block the escarpment track. Motor transport began to be a problem instead of a blessing and the Gold Coast artillerymen looked at their guns and then roundly cursed the weather. The column did two miles in twenty-four hours and everything mechanical simply drank the precious petrol. The engineers and the infantrymen pooled their resources. The road - it was really just a track across the downland up into the thick forest of wild fig trees - was methodically cleared of every obstacle. Bridges were repaired, old tanks were hauled into the bush and felled trees were broken up and moved.

Success was ahead. At 9.30 a.m. on May 20th the leading Company and a section of armoured cars ran into two battalions of enemy infantry and battery of guns and captured the whole lot.

It was just South of Hula and the total force surrendered including the commanding officer of the rearguard. This Italian Brigadier was very much on his dignity and did not like surrendering to a rather junior officer. He was told sharply that our force of 2,000 fighting troops was close behind and that he had better capitulate at once or else!!

The Brigadier surrendered with 1,700 men.

A party was left to guard the mob of prisoners and the rest pushed on, trekking along the waterlogged roads. That night the advance party entered Hula. There were only two platoons of them. The rest had been left behind to deal with the broken bridges. The small party had passed through a very trying time. The enemy had attempted to delay the advance by the usual methods. There were felled trees as before, and three huge pits, one particularly bad one on a hairpin bend. Somebody had a new idea and tore great strips of road metal from the road and threw it down the escarpment. Very troublesome in wet weather. But the engineers had done their work well, although at one stage the mobile advance column only managed nine miles before the sheets of never-ending rain and the deplorable roads brought them to a reluctant halt. The road was strewn with abandoned gear of every kind, left behind in the headlong flight of the enemy columns. There were mortars, machine guns, ammunition, mules alive and very dead, all the usual evidence of demoralization. Reduced in strength by the road conditions and the necessity for leaving platoons behind to look after each group of hundreds of prisoners (one party comprised fifty Italian Officers and 500 men) the mobile column went ahead and into Hula - two platoons strong.

In Hula there were two more enemy battalions and some cavalry personnel (minus horses) awaiting capture. Hula was just a muddy mess and when the Gold Coast troops arrived it was already 6.00 p.m. and getting dark, so perhaps the Italians may be forgiven for thinking that this mud-stained and worn force was some of their own rearguard coming in. They said their rearguard Commander was somewhere in front and they refused to believe that we had captured that worthy and dignified Brigadier already.

At Hula, also, the Italian Commander was reluctant to surrender to a junior officer but he was given a stark ultimatum which he agreed to with alacrity. The rest of that miserable night was spent organizing the disposal of the prisoners and collecting their arms. The remainder of our mobile column began to come in and a supply of petrol got through and the progress of the advance was ensured by the morning of the 22nd.

It was about this time that the Gold Coast Brigade suffered a sad loss. Lieutenant Manning who for many years had been Bandmaster of the Regiment was travelling in a car at the end of one of our transport columns when he and his two companions were ambushed and killed by Ethiopian Patriots who mistook them for Italians.

A quick reorganization was carried out at Hula and a small force of two companies, some armoured cars, some gunners and engineers moved forward to Uondo where some opposition was expected. Our mobile column met a small force of Italians coming from Uondo who immediately surrendered and seemed glad to do so.

On the morning of May 23rd we entered Uondo and were confronted by Italian armoured cars which appeared most hostile and seemed ready to open fire at any moment. The Italians simply could not believe that we had arrived so quickly and whilst they dithered the four South African armoured cars in our small force surrounded the enemy force – forcing it to surrender with no shots fired.

It was a splended haul at Uondo, 912 Italians and 812 Africans. The war material included about 100 large lorries and an arsenal full of rifles, besides a huge quantity of ammunition, medical and engineering stores and a large quantity of food; Uondo was just another native village, dirty and muddy and surrounded by tree-clad hills. It didn't seem worth all the trouble.

The Italian Officer commanding the Uondo troops explained to the Officer commanding the Gold Coast Battalion that he had a rheumatic heart, was feeling very ill, and therefore decided he would rather not fight.

'So,' said the Colonel with a twinkle, 'I put him in the front seat of my car and told him he was a very wise man.'

We had completed a memorable march. So had another Brigade, including King's African Rifles, who had started about the same time from Yavello, further west, and, travelling via Alge, joined the Gold Coast Brigade eventually at Uondo. That Brigade had no fighting to do but owing to the terrible road conditions it was a gruelling march. No motor transport could be used and the Brigade slogged along on foot for nineteen long and tiring days.

After Uondo we went on to Soddu and took over 10,000 prisoners from the King's African Rifles. At one time the three Gold Coast Battalions had 13,000 prisoners in their charge.

General Pursued

The Italian Divisional Commander commanding the 24th Italian Division on the Waddara front was General Pralormo. Well, when our troops entered Uondo they found that the General had skipped out the other side with 2,000 men six hours before – indeed, about 3.00 a.m. He made for the hills and was captured some considerable time afterwards. Before he left Uondo he told his force that as all the main roads were now closed he would go across country. He could only take the fittest with him, and besides his means of transport were limited.

Speaking of the battle of Waddara, General Pralormo declared afterwards that he knew he ought to have counter-attacked – but he could not trust his force. When he was eventually taken his 2,000 men were in very poor shape. For weeks they had been living mainly on cooked grass and dead mules, after General Gazzera could no longer drop food from the air. As the weary remnants of his Division marched into our lines after his surrender, Pralormo stood and took the salute.

One of my jobs as Adjutant of 3 G.C.R. at that time was to ensure that the General was properly looked after and that he had no means of escape.

I found him extremely pleasant and friendly and I relieved him of a superb Leica camera, in exchange for which I was able to give him a large bar of chocolate which for him was a great luxury.

Prisoners and Booty

From the beginning of the operations beyond Neghelli to the close at Uondo, the Gold Coast Brigade captures included the following:

European prisoners	1,176
Africans	3,844
Armoured cars	7
Guns	8
Heavy machine guns	48
Light machine guns	147
Rifles	7,000
Lorries, abandoned but serviceable	118

Finally, three miles beyond Uondo there is, or was, a bridge on the road to Dalle. The Italians blew it up. Across the gap, on May 22nd, the Brigadier commanding the King's African Rifles who had taken Dalle from the North, and the Colonel of the Gold Coast Battalion who had pushed through to Uondo, shook hands.

And that is how the junction was effected between the one part of the East African Force in the north that had fought the Italians from Addis Ababa and the other who had driven the enemy before them from the south. That handshake meant that the job in Abyssinia was nearly done.

The description of the period after the battle of Waddara until the early part of September 1941 highlights the difficulties under which we were operating. The story which I now relate was written either by myself as Adjutant or by the late Sir Michael Gass (the Intelligence Officer), I forget which. The fighting was over but much remained to be done and the situation between Waddara and Addis Ababa was chaotic. The 'Shifta' still active, the patriots, Italian prisoners of war and enormous quantities of enemy weapons and war materials all had to be dealt with and 3 G.C.R. was given this daunting task which was carried out successfully in appalling weather conditions. All the officers and British Non-Commissioned Officers mentioned were either Company Commanders or Platoon Commanders in 3 G.C.R..

Battalion headquarters were at Didessa as was the Movement Control post which controlled all movement on the road between Iubdo and Baco.

Had it not been for the continual rain the system would have worked like clockwork but as it was, certain stretches of road, particularly that between Didessa and Lechenti, became impassable with the result that while the prisoners could not be evacuated their rations would not be got forward to them. The run of thirty-one miles from Didessa to Lechenti took seven hours; from Iubdo to Ghimbe – a distance of sixty miles –

took two days, in spite of the fact that our troops, a Field Company and gangs of prisoners were working continuously on the roads.

Communication between all the staging camps and Battalion H.Q. was maintained by wireless telegraphy and by the same means the movements of convoys was controlled by the Traffic Control Point at Didessa. The occasional breakdown of the wireless at a staging camp resulted in all sorts of complications; large convoys would arrive in the dark, unexpected and laden with prisoners who had to be counted in the dark (a performance which even in daylight proved too much for the patience of the average European). Or, when a wireless breakdown silenced the movement control officer, large convoys would meet on the narrow ledge of a patched-up road which led up the escarpment. However, in spite of these inevitable hitches, the evacuation continued steadily.

'D' Company, being the furthest away from the rest of the Battalion, suffered more than others from the uncertainty of ration supplies, and when a large number of prisoners arrived and cleared them of their remaining P.O.W. rations it frequently took a week before further supplies could reach them. Naturally their difficulties in obtaining petrol and dieseline were no less. For their evacuation they had to rely entirely on captured ten-ton diesels driven by prisoners of war. Captain Daly was very short of Europeans and the work of running the prisoner of war camp, providing escorts for convoys and arranging for the evacuation of odd units such as Patriots and the 2/6 King's African Rifles meant very hard work for them.

Captain Barrett was more fortunate in that the road between Ghimbe and Didessa was seldom impassable, but 'C' company were probably better off than any others as they had no prisoner of war camp to look after and were not in wireless communication with Battalion. Captain Grant's platoons were spread out along the road between Ghimbe and Didessa on the task of maintaining various drifts and bridge approaches. 2/Lieutenant Powell and Sergeant Caull lived in solitary state on the Western and Eastern ends of the Didessa River escarpments where they were in telephonic communication with each other. They ensured that on their section, which included a very dangerous and precipitous piece of road as well as a single track temporary bridge, one-way traffic was strictly enforced.

The notorious prisoner of war camp at Didessa was run by Headquarter Company who arrived somewhat later than the rest of the Battalion, having been impressed into a road gang *en route* from Baco. As is usual on such occasions the European personnel of this company of specialists gradually disappeared. They were later discovered in the following posts: Lieutenants Marsh and Smit had taken over Italian Brigade Group, Lieutenant Thompson was run to earth in the traffic control point, Didessa, while 2/Lieutenant Merlen had got as far as Lechenti where he too had a control post. In fact after Captain Favard (Rastas) had left to take up a post in Division Captain Moore (Sainty) was left with only one officer and two British N.C.O.s with which to run Headquarter Company.

At Lechenti the drudgery of looking after Italians was occasionally relieved by shooting on the part of the local inhabitants. Sergeant Major Beer was shot at but fortunately was not hit. However, amongst other people who found themselves acting as targets for the local marksmen, a certain Regimental Motor Transport Sergeant was unfortunate enough to be shot through the thigh. Lechenti was a town of fair size, as towns go in this part of the world, and there was the usual trouble of friction between the civilian population and our troops, as well as many cases of drunkenness. On top of all this Captain Packham had to deal with quite the worst bit of road in the whole area. Heavy rain daily converted the black cotton-soil into a quagmire which swallowed numerous lorry loads of stone without showing the slightest sign of improvement.

Shortly after our arrival in the area all services of 11 Division were withdrawn and, as they were not relieved by 12 Division or by 24 Gold Coast Brigade, reliefs had to be provided out of the Battalion's personnel - already very much under strength. Major French together with four other officers were occupied by courts of enquiry at Ghimbe and indeed the number of Europeans available for work on evacuation of prisoners was reduced to a bare minimum.

'D' Company had a variety of extra tasks with which they had to deal. They had to arrange for the transport of the 2/6 King's African Rifles who were to return to Addis Ababa after completing their operations from the Sudan border. Similar arrangements had to be made for a large body of Abyssinian Patriots, and Company Sergeant Major Butchart had to go out further west with one platoon to make contact with a Field Company of the Sudan Defence Force and to obtain from them a report on the possibility of bridging the Indina River or of repairing the ferry over it.

Company Quartermaster Sergeant Bamberger was sent out with transport to collect about 300 sick prisoners of war, women and children and though expected back in three days there was no news of him until he turned up again a week later. An hour after setting out he had been held up by a cloudburst and the road continued to get worse and worse – three lorries overturned and an equal number returned with broken springs. The rations had run out and the sick prisoners were in a very sorry state when they arrived in Ghimbe.

By August 16th some 3,300 prisoners of war had been evacuated as far as Baco; a further 1,874 were in staging camps *en route* for Baco, leaving only 370 at Iubdo, consequently the remainder of Battalion H.Q. the divisional Signals and the Traffic Control post moved from Didessa to Baco. The Commanding Officer and myself (Adjutant) were already there with 'C' Company and two platoons of 'B' Company. Lieutenants Marsh and Smit were also established some eight miles east of Baco where they continued to outshine the East African Army Service Corps in their management of the Supplies.

The concentration of the Battalion to Baco took place gradually as the evacuation of the western staging camps was completed, and on August 24th 'A' Company left Ghimbe for Baco, their duties being taken over by 'D' Company. The road Eastwards from Didessa was by this time so bad that lorries could only be got through by unloading them and pushing them through one at a time. It took Captain Barrett the better part of four days to cover the 120 miles to Baco.

No sooner had 'A' Company arrived than a message was received at Baco stating that despite all efforts to save it the small bridge over the River Didessa had been washed away as the result of a sudden rise of the river. Three days later another message reached Battalion H.Q. informing them that the bridge over the river twenty-two miles East of Ghimbi had also been washed away by floods. Thus all troops West of Didessa were cut off completely. This made it difficult to see how the evacuation of these areas could be completed in time for the Battalion to be ready to move to Addis Ababa on September 10th as ordered by 12th Division.

However, 'A' Company being already in Baco were able to move and on August 30th they left for Addis Ababa by road whence to proceed to Adama by rail. They were to take over from the 12th King's African Rifles the duties guarding the prisoner of war camp there and of protecting the station and railway line.

Meanwhile the evacuation of the 3,000 prisoners at Baco was nearing completion and with the arrival of Headquarter Company only half of

'B' Company and 'D' Company were left at Lechenti and on the west of the Didessa River respectively.

At the Didessa River, where both bridges were unsafe or washed away, Captain Moore and Lieutenant MacArthur were at considerable personal risk ferrying rations across the flooded stream on a raft of empty petrol drums.

The Battalion's task in this area was once again the evacuation of prisoners and salvage. After our experiences in Soddu we were hardly looking forward to the job with relish, but there we had at least been responsible for the capture of most of the prisoners; this time, however, we had to do the dirty work of operations in which we had no hand, which made the work doubly tedious.

The enemy personnel and material which we were to collect and evacuate had fallen into allied hands as a result of the surrender to the Belgian Forces of the Commander-in-Chief's army. This enemy force, which included such oddments as naval men from Massaua and troops who had escaped from Keren, had retreated Westwards from Addis Ababa when the city fell into our hands. Pursued by Units of the Nigeria Regiment and South African Forces they continued to withdraw westwards leaving a series of bridge and road demolitions in their wake. Eventually, however, they came in contact with troops from the Belgian Congo who together with the 2/6 King's African Rifles had advanced into Abyssinia from the Sudan. The Abyssinian Patriots were also operating in conjunction with our troops and in fact the Italians found themselves surrounded. They therefore came to terms with the Belgians and surrendered to them at Dembidolo early in July. All prisoners of war and material which fell into allied hands as a result of this surrender had to be transported to Addis Ababa by us.

> The actual number of prisoners of war in the area was as follows: 10 Generals, 2,982 Italian officers and other ranks, and 1,700 Native troops. Amongst the large quantities of salvage were 2 armoured cars. 120 lorries, 18 guns and many machine guns besides bridging materials, etc.

The road from Baco continued Westwards as a narrow earth road which became impassable after heavy rain and at the best of times was only wide enough for one-way traffic. At this time of the year (July) the rains were still at their height so that the road was always bad and hampered all our efforts at getting the evacuation completed quickly. Many bridges had been destroyed, and though repaired by our engineers they were in some cases washed away by the flooded rivers and effectively prevented any movement of prisoners.

We were to contact the Belgians at Iubdo, some 190 miles west of Baco and only eighty miles from the Sudan border. The prisoners of war were to be handed over to us there and they would then become our responsibility.

The 190 miles from Iubdo to Baco was therefore divided into four sections with a staging camp at the end of each section. Each staging camp was provided with its own transport for convoying prisoners of war and one company was to look after each camp. Briefly the system worked as follows. Captain Daly collected prisoners from the Belgians at Iubdo and sent them back to the next camp at Ghimbe some sixty miles further East. At Ghimbe Captain Barrett took them over and in turn sent them on to the camp at Didessa where the prisoners came into the unsympathetic clutches of Captain Favard. Thence the prisoners were sent on to Lechenti where Captain Packham had his Company and finally they arrived at Baco whence they were accumulated to await evacuation to Addis Ababa when transport became available. Sergeant O'Connor had to deal with this camp almost single-handed until Captain Maddison returned from hospital and took over.

It was during this rather hectic period when all the Companies of the 3 G.C.R. were extremely actively employed on the administration of prisoners of war and their evacuation of P.W. Camps that Battalion H.Q. 3 G.C.R. moved to Soddu.

Soddu was a lovely village in a valley surrounded by mountains and everywhere lush green grass and beautiful wild flowers. We in Battalion H.Q. were in wireless communication with all our companies and were able to direct the overall plans for prisoner of war evacuation.

There was always a food problem. We were, of course, mainly able to use the Italian rations but very often these rations had to be moved long distances over quite frightful roads. It was still the rainy season and this made the problem even worse.

My recollections of Soddu was that it was a pleasant rest, a lovely village in superb scenery. Colonel Tank Western insisted that the H.Q. wireless was manned throughout the night and this meant that I (Adjutant), the Intelligence Officer (Michael Gass) and the Signals Officer (Swampy Marsh) had to take turns for a two-hour watch. I found this chore troublesome and irritating and for weeks on end the three of us never had a proper night's rest.

I visited a Coptic church in Soddu and stole a silver chalice which I subsequently returned to its rightful place after the war at my late wife's insistence.

Thus ended a peaceful period but we always had to be on the look-out for 'Shiftas', a villainous collection of cut-throats only interested in loot and murder. It was now mid-September, the Prisoners of War had all been evacuated and orders were received from Higher Command for the Battalion to move to Addis Ababa.

I remember the thrill and excitement of entering the capital and to be told that the Emperor Haile Selassie was again on his throne. It was a time of great rejoicing and although my memory is a little dim after nearly fifty years I do remember some lighter moments.

There was a night club in Addis called 'The Two Piss Pots' – it sticks in my mind because the 'Piss Pots' were positioned above the door. The ladies were Italian and extremely beautiful and the Gold Coast Brigade Officers used to visit the establishment nightly for dancing and whatever!

Addis was not all that peaceful and rifle shots and other explosions were continuous throughout the nights and we carried arms at all times. It was during this time in Addis that I met and had lunch with General Sammy Butler at the British Legation. He was asking for young Officers from the Gold Coast Brigade to be seconded for a limited period to form and train a new Ethiopian Army. I was one of the Officers selected and my initial reaction was one of enthusiasm. I was then 28 years old, a Captain with a prospect of Command of an Ethiopian Battalion, promotion to Lieutenant-Colonel and a huge salary.

However, my Divisional Commander General Godwin Austen and my Brigadier, Piggy Richards, were both lukewarm on the prospects and advised against it. With hindsight I believe they were right and it turned out that Abyssinia became a backwater after the campaign was over and I would have missed all the fun and excitement which I was fortunate to take part in later in the War.

I have now only a vague recollection of the few weeks we spent in Addis but I do remember that it was a time of great exultation; after all we had won a notable victory, almost the first success the Allies had achieved since the beginning of the war, and that with a force many times smaller both in numbers and weapons than the Italians.

Generale di Brigata Emanuele Beraudo di Pralormo. Africa Orientale 1940. Commander 24th Italian Division at battle of Waddara. Captured by 3rd Gold Coast Regiment.

Brigadier C. E. M. Richards, C.B.E., D.S.O., M.C., Commander Gold Coast Brigade, East African Campaign 1940–1941.

Wajir Fort (Northern Frontier District, Kenya) from where the Gold Coast Brigade set off for their spectacular advance, destruction and pursuit of the Italian forces in Somaliland and Abyssinia.

The author as Adjutant 3rd Gold Coast Regiment at Wajir Fort, 1940.

2nd Gold Coast Regiment takes Burro Erillo (Italian Somaliland) March 1941.

Gold Coast troops patrolling on the Kenya–Somaliland border – February 1941.

1st Sierra Leone Regiment operations in the Kaladan Valley, 1944.

The dense bamboo jungle in which we were operating in the Kaladan Valley.

Troops of 81st West African Division during operations on the Kaladan River, 1944.

Major General F. J. Loftus-Tottenham, D.S.O., G.O.C., 81st West African Division R.W.A.F.F.

Lance Corporal Bobo Jumbo, M.M., with the Japanese sword captured from an enemy officer on Point 887 and given to the author – Christmas 1944.

Myself when commanding
1st Sierra Leone Regiment R.W.A.F.F., Kaladan 1944.

Chapter 6

A Summary of the East African Campaign

The following is the summary of the East African campaign as described by the *East African Standard*'s special correspondent, Mr George Kinnear.

It would seem that a short summary of the whole East African campaign in Abyssinia and Somaliland might give the (general) reader some idea of the successful manner in which by a pan-African effort, a remarkable military task was brought to a swift and triumphant conclusion and to show it to have been one of the most outstanding achievements in military history.

At no time did the British Forces total more than 20,000 infantry; at no time did they have more than 68 field guns. Owing to the difficulties of maintenance, it was never possible to employ more than 3 Brigades (about 8,000 infantry) at any one time in offensive operations against the enemy. And yet our troops overcame 96,000 infantry with 403 guns, and destroyed an army totalling 170,000 fighting men.

In less than six months they drove the enemy from an area approximately as large as England, Scotland, Wales, Ireland, France, Spain and Italy combined, and the main advance covered a distance as great as that from London to the Caspian, from Ireland to Newfoundland or from Washington to San Francisco.

The effort which secured these well-nigh incredible results was essentially pan-African. The great majority of the troops were recruited from the Union of South Africa, the Rhodesians and Western and Eastern African territories. The only troops drawn from other sources were Imperial troops forming Signal and other specialist services and some Indian Mountain Batteries. The Imperials carried out their duties with the cheerfulness and endurance which is so likely to be overlooked because it is expected, while the Indians fully lived up to the glorious traditions of the Indian Army.

From a brief study of the campaign and with the consideration given to the vast distances covered and the speed of advance that was maintained despite lack of water and bad communications, it is clear that throughout every phase the success of the forward troops was entirely dependent on the efficient working of the services maintaining them. The provision of rations, water, ammunition, petrol and all the other requirements of the fighting battalions never failed. The problems that faced the staff with no railways, no base port facilities outside Kenya Territory, and lines of communication thousands of miles in length, were all overcome by efficient planning and the devotion to duty of those detailed to carry out the plan.

Among all those who created success in the back areas special mention must be made of the M.T. drivers and the Road Construction Companies. Working in indescribable conditions of heat, dust and flies, and later in mud and rain, and always in discomfort, personnel from these units maintained unfailing cheerfulness throughout their long hours of work. Staff and women's services and others left in Kenya, often short-handed and frequently bored by lack of action, contributed to our services by carrying out their tasks with stolid determination.

The Juba Onwards

The campaign which resulted in the final defeat of the Italians opposed to the East African Force opened with the Battle of the Juba River in February 1941. In this Battle the 12th (African) Division commanded by Major-General A. R. Godwin-Austen, C.B., O.B.E., M.C., and consisting of the 1st South African Brigade, the 22nd (East African) and the 24th (Gold Coast) Infantry Brigades, forced a crossing of the river, and having established bridgeheads on the far bank, enabled the 11th ('A') Division to be slipped through and to take up the advance into Italian Somaliland.

In this initial battle the 12th ('A') Division showed their superiority to the Italian troops in no mean style, and it was their overwhelming success in this crucial battle that started the rot in the Italian Army and made the remainder of the campaign possible.

A New Phase

After the capture of Addis Ababa the campaign entered a new phase. The 1st (South African) Brigade assisted the Sudan Forces to open the road to Asmara and the North. Their brilliant victory after heavy fighting at Dessia cleared the way for the capture of Amba Alagi, which resulted in opening the road and led to the final surrender of the Viceroy.

The 22nd Brigade struck south and during the Battle of the Lakes captured Sciasci Amanna. The 12th ('A') Division attacked from the south from the neighbourhood of Neghelli and Yavello, while the 22nd Brigade reinforced by the 23rd (Nigerian) Brigade and the 2nd (South African) Brigade cut the enemy's line of retreat to Jimma.

Thus it came about that when the 12th ('A') Division, after Waddara, perhaps the most arduous battle of the campaign, forced the enemy to retreat, there was no way of escape left open and the entire personnel of four Italian Divisions were killed, captured or dispersed.

The Battle of the Lakes was noteworthy for the tactical skill employed by the 11th and 12th ('A') Divisions which resulted in such a sweeping vistory; and also for the success of our East African and West African native soldiers against Italian national and colonial forces.

Omo Overcome

Following the Battle of the Lakes and their retreat from the Soddu area, the enemy took refuge behind the line of River Omo. Swollen by heavy rains, and with its far bank defended by prepared enemy positions, the river was indeed a formidable proposition. This obstacle, however, did not impose any great delay. With the ability which is characteristic of our native forces through all the varying conditions of warfare which have been met with, King's African Rifles and West African Frontier Forces units forced crossing in two places and drove the enemy back in headlong flight.

The occupation of Juma followed, and with the crossing of the Didessa River by the Nigerian Brigade the campaign was virtually ended. The Italian High Command, hemmed in by Belgian and African troops, bombed from the air, and with scattered forces continually harried by Patriots and depressed by the condition of their continuous retreat, surrendered.

It must be remembered that owing to the energetic action of the South African Air Force, air superiority was gained at the very outset, and our forces did not have to contend with any but intermittent hostile action from the air. It must also be remembered that the majority of our native forces were not seasoned troops. Nigerian and Gold Coast units, unaccustomed to cold and damp, fought from hot dusty bush to wet cold highlands and East African natives, the majority of whom were unsophisticated and unaccustomed to any activity other than the peaceful existence of their village life, fought side-by-side with them. Whatever the conditions and whatever the weapons employed against them, all our troops carried their tasks with cheerfulness, energy, courage and complete disregard for their own safety and comfort.

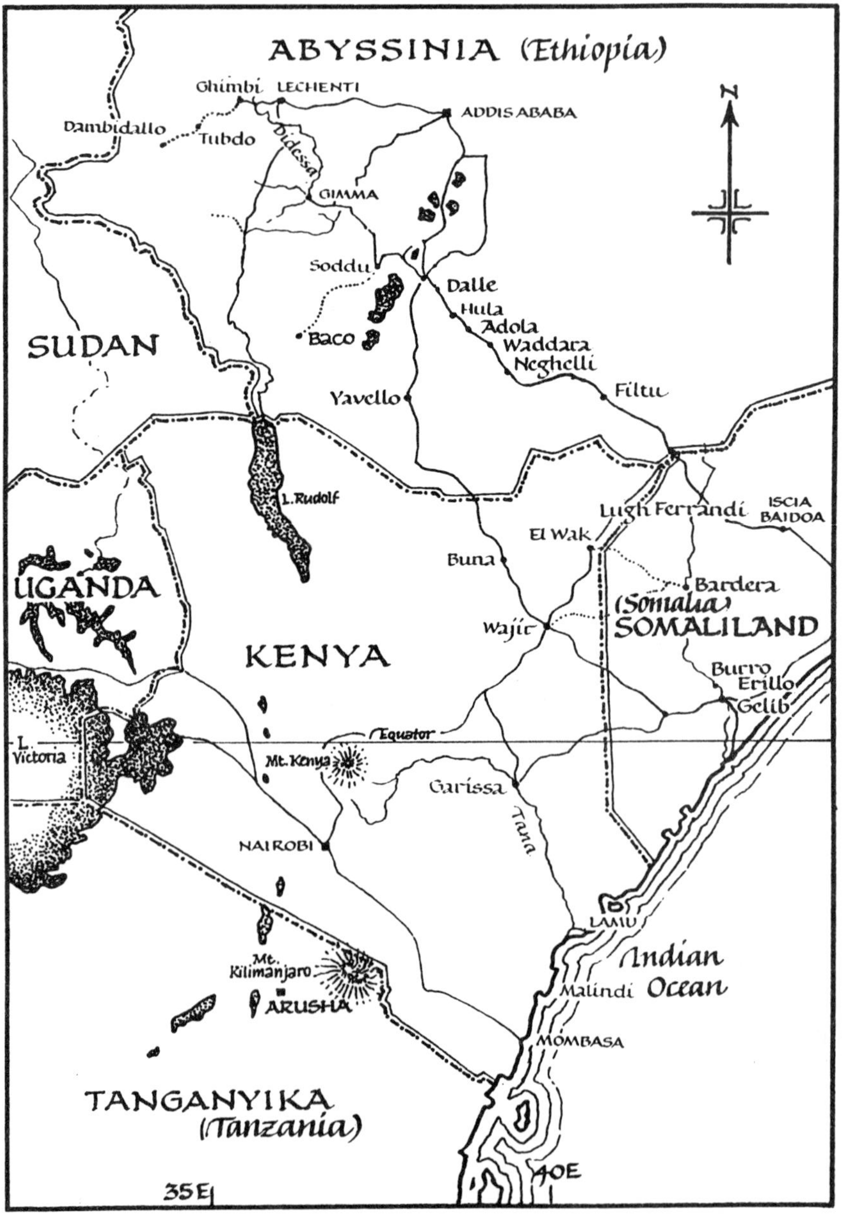
ABYSSINIA (Ethiopia)
Ghimbi
LECHENTI
ADDIS ABABA
Dambidallo
Tubdo
Didessa
GIMMA
Soddu
Dalle
Hula
Adola
Waddara
Neghelli
Baco
Filtu
Yavello
SUDAN
L. Rudolf
Lugh Ferrandi
ISCIA BAIDOA
El Wak
Buna
Bardera
(Somalia)
SOMALILAND
Wajir
UGANDA
KENYA
Burro Erillo
Gelib
Equator
L. Victoria
Mt. Kenya
Garissa
Tana
NAIROBI
LAMU
Indian Ocean
Mt. Kilimanjaro
Malindi
ARUSHA
MOMBASA
TANGANYIKA
(Tanzania)
35E
40E
N

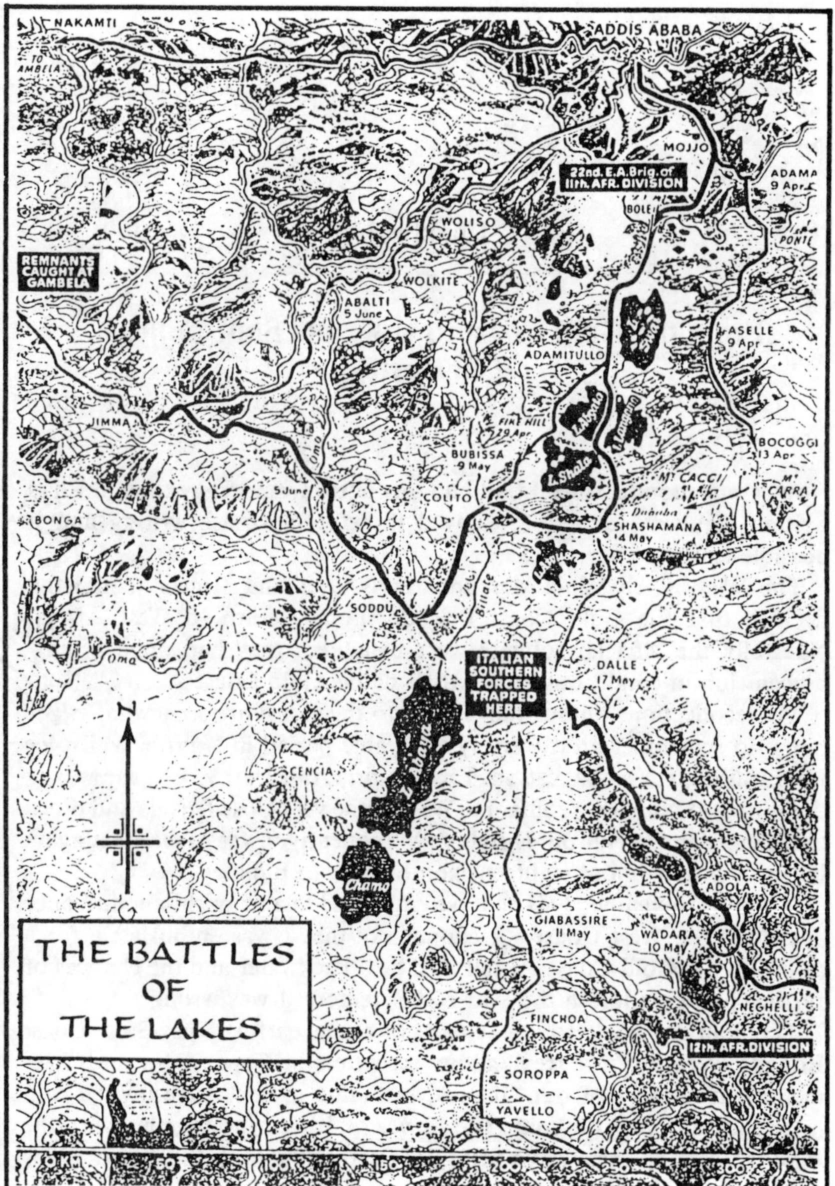

THE BATTLES OF THE LAKES

Chapter 7

From the Gold Coast to U.K. and Staff College, Camberley

Now it was months since I had had any letter from Peggy though I had written regularly to her. I resolved therefore to cease writing and if possible to forget her.

The War in Abyssinia was apparently over and Higher Command decided that the Gold Coast Brigade should return to West Africa. Naturally the African soldiers were delighted: they had done a magnificent job in conditions unlike their native Gold Coast.

My recollections on our move back to the Coast are somewhat vague but I do remember an extremely enjoyable period in Nairobi whilst we were waiting for embarkation. I met a girl, Ann Duthy, and she was in the First Aid Nursing Yeomanry. We became very close friends and dined and danced in the Nairobi Hotels very frequently. I was to meet her again but only briefly about eighteen months later in India.

It was in November 1941 that we embarked in a troopship bound once again for the West Coast – I cannot say that I was enthusiastic for a return to the Gold Coast – I felt it to be a backwater and the chances of further participation in the War rather remote. I was wrong.

The journey back to the Coast was uneventful. The Gold Coast Brigade were given a tremendous reception in Cape Town and I remember a number of our Officers, including myself, were invited to a huge cocktail party on board the *Prince of Wales* who together with the *Repulse* were on their way to the Far East. Sadly both these great ships were sunk by the Japanese only a few weeks later. We reached the Coast and our African troops were given a reasonably long period of leave with their families.

Life in Accra during this period was back to peacetime standards - we played polo, cricket and golf and there were the usual evening drink parties.

Colonel Tank Western, my Commanding Officer who I had served as Adjutant both in the formation and training of the Battalion and throughout the Abyssinian campaign, saw fit to promote a part-time Officer to the rank of Major in the only vacancy available at that time. I was naturally incensed at this decision which I considered to be grossly unfair and asked for an interview with the Brigadier (Piggy Richards) to make a formal complaint.

The Brigadier fully supported my case and offered me the post of Deputy Assistant Quarter Master General at Brigade Headquarters with promotion to Major. I had served with Tank Western for a very long time. He was a fine trainer of troops and personally a courageous man but, although our relationship was for the most part friendly, I found him at times difficult.

I moved to Brigade H.Q. and took over the duties of D.A.A. & Q.M.G. which involved matters concerning the administration of all units in the Brigade. I enjoyed the work and the Brigade Major, Frank Coulson, and I became great friends. I remember the Brigade Staff 'set up' to have been efficient and happy.

I, of course, got to know Brigadier Richards (Piggy) very well - I shared a bungalow with him and in fact served as Aide-de-Camp to him in addition to my other duties. He was a great fighting Commander and he was enormously well liked by all units in the Gold Coast Brigade.

It was at this time and after many months that I had a letter from Peggy. She had escaped from Singapore just before its fall, was in England and had joined the Wrens in Portsmouth. She admitted having had another boyfriend but it was over and could we meet again if I ever got back to the U.K.? I felt rather lukewarm about our relationship at this time and wrote to her on those lines.

It was a month or two later that I received some splendid news. I had been selected to attend a course at the Staff College, Camberley. This of course meant some leave at Spennithorne first and I was delighted.

At the same time, the Gold Coast Brigade received orders to move to the Gambia for reasons that were unknown at that time. I accompanied the Brigade to Gambia after I handed over my Brigade duties to my successor and there awaited a passage to the U.K. Those few weeks in Gambia were very enjoyable and every day Colonel Tank Western and I hired a native boat which we rowed ourselves on the Gambia River collecting most beautiful oysters which we extracted from sunken trees on the edge of the River.

At last the orders for my passage to the U.K. arrived and I was to fly to Freetown and embark on a Troopship bound for the U.K. I recollect that the voyage home was uneventful. There were a lot of R.A.F. pilot officers from Australia - not very friendly - who delighted in calling the few British Officers like myself 'Pommies'.

Life at home in the U.K. was pretty austere though I was lucky to get a small extra ration of petrol for being on leave from abroad. I decided to write to Peggy and suggest visiting her in Portsmouth where she was stationed and doing a tour of duty with the Wrens.

At that first meeting I knew that I still loved her and in fact we got unofficially engaged. I then persuaded my mother to come with me to Portsmouth to meet her. My mother was wonderful on this occasion and in fact fully supported my choice. When I reached home after my visit to Portsmouth, I was as much in love as ever with Peggy but there was a nagging doubt in my mind as to whether we should be married. She was much younger than I was, she had lived an entirely different life to anything I could offer her at Spennithorne, and I could not help wondering if I could make her happy. I spent many days of indecision and finally decided that I should return to Portsmouth and break off the engagement. To this day I vividly remember that our last meeting was particularly sad for us both - I was still in love with Peggy and made a poor showing of my reasons for 'walking out on her'. I left Portsmouth by train, desolate and unhappy, and on reaching Waterloo I queued for a taxi. In those wartime days we had to share and my companion was a very pretty girl going somewhere in my direction - I just had to tell her my troubles and what had happened. She was very understanding and sympathetic and told me that it was not an unknown occurrence and that I should try to forget it very soon but I did not!

I had three months leave at Spennithorne to come before the start of the Staff College course and I cannot say that this period was at all happy - I was totally unable to put the matter of my broken engagement aside and forget about it so in this troubled frame of mind I arrived in late May 1942 at Minley Manor for the 9th Staff War Course.

The previous evening I had stayed at my London Club (The R.A.G.)

and there met an old friend (Colonel Hugh Bellamy, nicknamed the 'Laughing Horse') and we decided to go to a night club ('The Bag of Nails'). We got pretty drunk I remember, and it took the first two days at Minley before I could make any sense at all.

I found the Staff College course extremely hard going and although I was one of the few students who had seen active service, the fact that I had been so long in Africa meant that I was out of date with the methods and thinking of modern war in Europe. We worked in syndicates and my Instructor was a young South African (Lieutenant-Colonel Ian McKenzie). He was an awfully nice person – he saw I was worried and out of my depth and visited me in my room every evening mainly with the object of raising morale and helping me. There were times in the middle of the course when I felt that I was doing so badly that I might even fail the course; however, as on many occasions before and after in my life, friends came to my rescue and I was persuaded to take things less seriously.

This advice proved totally right and though my final grading was not spectacular I finished the course in fair fettle. I said my early days at the Staff College were very unhappy – I was unable to forget Peggy Wilson and the way in which I had let her down – I was still in love with her and in my unsettled state I decided to telephone her in Portsmouth asking her to meet me again – she agreed and a meeting was arranged.

The following day I changed my mind and made a final break with her causing further unhappiness and disillusionment to her.

I have never forgotten this episode in my life.

I made a lot of friends many of whom I saw later in the War. It was high Summer and I played a lot of cricket, golf and tennis at weekends. I played cricket regularly for the Staff College on the lovely Minley Ground and on one memorable occasion went in first to bat with Bill Edrich (Middlesex and England). Bill made 100 whilst I made 20 and I remember being irritated as he was always able to steal a single at the end of each over and thereby get the batting!

The syndicate discussions were great fun and very interesting; however, for the reasons given above, I found I could only take a limited part. General Sir Alan Cunningham, my Army Commander in East Africa, was the Commandant and I was able to meet him during the course and reminisce on the East African campaign.

Though I felt I had not done particularly well, I managed to achieve 'Passed Staff College' and, in addition, was confident that I could do any

Grade 2 staff job tolerably well. Amongst friends and acquaintances who were with me on this course were the late Major Peter James, Rifle Brigade, the late General Basil Fugster, Irish Guards, the late Lieutenant-Colonel Jocylin Gurney, Welsh Guards, who was in fact in my syndicate and shared a room with me. After the Staff College course we were all given a period of leave and went to await a new posting.

I spent my leave at Spennithorne with my mother. Petrol and food was strictly rationed and life was pretty quiet. I was very anxious to return to my own Regiment (the 43rd) and did not want to be sent abroad again. I therefore asked for an interview with the Military Secretary Branch of the War Office and was granted an interview with Major Peter Wrightson who was the GII in that department and an old friend. Unfortunately, I had been selected for a GII appointment in South-East Asia Command in India and apparently this posting could not be altered and I must make the best of it.

It was now Autumn 1941 and I received a Warning Order to be prepared for Embarkation Orders at short notice. We were required to report to the Reuben Hotel in London at certain times of the day so I made the Army and Navy Club in Pall Mall my base and within a week the orders came. I well remember the train journey from London to Liverpool. We left at about 9.00 p.m. and travelled through the night in complete darkness. The train was packed full with Officers posted to South-East Asia Command and it was a dreary, cold and miserable journey.

The ship on which we embarked the next morning was the P. & O. Liner *Strathmore*, a cruise liner which had been fitted up as a Wartime troopship - I cannot remember much of that voyage to India but it was a very large convoy and we were well protected by destroyers of the Royal Navy. I do remember, however, on one occasion being attacked by enemy aircraft in the Suez Canal area and the bombs falling close to the *Strathmore*.

We reached Bombay in late 1941 where I, and a number of Staff Officers who had been my companions on the ship, boarded a train bound for Delhi. I found that I had been appointed a Deputy Assistant Adjutant General (D.A.A.G.) in the newly formed South-East Asia Command. Our offices were in Old Delhi with living quarters close to the Officers' Mess and conditions and food were tolerable. There were two other D.A.A.G.s with a Brigadier (Ridley Thompson), nicknamed Tidley, as our immediate superior officer.

To this day, I have never understood why we were here, in Old Delhi thousands of miles from the Burma War front, and I speak the truth when I say there was nothing to do. I remember the Brigadier in desperation gave me the job of constructing a tennis court for the Officers in Old Delhi. Orde Wingate turned up one day on his way into Burma - I had a drink with him and thought he was rude and uncouth.

After about a month we were called to the large Conference Hall in New Delhi and were addressed by Admiral Lord Louis Mountbatten who had just arrived as the Supremo of South-East Asia Command. I was greatly impressed by his address to us and it was a tremendous morale raiser.

At this time, there had been a great and memorable battle in the Arakan when the Japanese had come near to defeating us. Its name was the Battle of the Admin Box when one of the Divisional Generals (General Messervy) had narrowly escaped capture in his pyjamas. The 15th Corps, who were directing this battle, had become short of Grade II Staff Officers and I was fortunate to be chosen to fly into the battle area of 15th Corps to take over a D.A.A.G. appointment.

Again I was lucky because General Sir George Giffard, the Army Commander 11th Army Group, required an Aide-de-Camp to travel with him to the battle area of the Arakan. I had known General Giffard for many years when he was Inspector General to the Royal West African Frontier Force, so this opportunity to visit the battle area with him was a particularly exciting prospect.

We left Delhi Airport in a private aircraft reserved for the Commander-in-Chief and I well remember that flight for we flew parallel to Mount Everest and not a great distance from it and the sight of those fantastic Himalayan peaks was unforgettable. There was a night stop at Comilla which was the H.Q. of the 14th Army. I was introduced to General Bill Slim, the Commander-in-Chief, and was extremely impressed with his friendliness to a junior and unknown Officer. The following day we flew into the battle zone and to H.Q. XV Corps, at Bawli Bazaar. The Battle of the Admin Box was over and XV Corps, who had withheld the Japanese attack, was licking its wounds.

I was introduced to my brother Officers on the Corps staff and learnt something of the work I was required to do. On my first day I accompanied General Giffard over the battle area and we visited the Ngakyedavk Pass where a great battle had been waged and won. We visited many units and it was pleasing to find morale very high. A

Battalion of my own Regiment, the Oxford Bucks Light Infantry, were in the line and I was happy to see the Commanding Officer Lieutenant Colonel, Peter Metcalfe (Wooster), who was an old friend.

I was with H.Q. 15 Corps for about two months, the work was not arduous and I much enjoyed visiting the units and made many friends. But now a message was received from 11 Army Group in Delhi for me to return. I did not want to leave XV Corps, and great efforts were made by the Corps Commander, General Sir Philip Christerson, and Senior Staff to keep me. However, higher authority prevailed and I was ordered to return.

I only remember a part of the journey back to Delhi and that was in a Dutch boat from Chittagong to Calcutta across the Bay of Bengal. I made friends with the Captain and we drank Schnapps till far into the night. I boarded a plane in Calcutta bound for Delhi and remember a fair amount of discomfort on a two-day-long journey in extremely hot weather.

Back in Old Delhi I found life much the same as before, extremely boring office work and on many days not a paper in my 'in-basket' and never a decision to take.

After about a month I was asked by my Brigadier if I would like to go to Ceylon as 11 Army Group's Staff Representative on Lord Louis Mountbatten's Headquarters (South-East Asia Command). I accepted this appointment with very great enthusiasm as I felt that nothing could be as soul-destroying as life in Old Delhi.

Once again I suffered the long hot railway and boat journey from Delhi to Ceylon and eventually arrived at Advanced H.Q. 11 Army Group in Kandy. The Offices and Mess had been newly built and were very comfortable, indeed palatial. We were located in Peradinya Gardens and it was a veritable 'Garden of Eden' – a dreamland if ever there was one! Lord Louis's H.Q. was beautifully laid out with restaurants, a dance hall and every amenity that could possibly be required for a long war.

I was a GII liaison between the 'A' Branch of 11 Army Group and South-East Asia Command and I could not say that the work was arduous. On many days my 'in-basket' was entirely empty and I was impatient to get to a lovely little golf course close by where I had many friends on the South-East Asia Command H.Q. Gerry Waites, Lord Louis's Sports Officer, was a particular friend and a great golfing companion. I also had a number of girl friends from the Wrens who worked in Lord Louis's H.Q. Audrey Oliver was a very special girlfriend and we went on a local leave together to Nurelya where Lord Louis had a leave camp.

I suppose I must have been in this idyllic place for about six months. Cricket, hockey and golf and the ladies were all I thought about and the War passed me by, until one day when strolling in Peredinya Gardens, I again met the Army Commander, General Sir George Gifford. He said, 'Straubenzee, what are you doing here?' I explained. He said, 'We urgently want Officers of the Royal West African Frontier Force for appointments in Burma and I shall see that you are posted there as soon as possible.'

This was a bombshell and I was not over enthusiastic. I awaited the proposed new posting with some trepidation and soon knew that I was to go as Second-in-Command to the 1 Sierra Leone Regiment in 81 West African Division Royal West African Frontier Force somewhere in Burma Jungle. I asked, and was granted, a period of leave before my new posting and I decided to go to a leave camp in Southern India – Arranmore in the Nilgri Hills. This was a really lovely place very like the Scottish Highlands in some ways.

The leave camp was run by a Lady Stow who I subsequently heard was a great friend of my cousin General Sir Casimir van Straubenzee. I was made most welcome and the days passed too quickly. There were some kindred spirits and we played golf every day on a most beautiful eighteen hole course.

Chapter 8

Burma (Kaladan) Operations (Phase II) September 1944 – January 1945

Soon, I was on my way again, another agonizing journey by train across India to Calcutta. It was here that I dumped all my heavy luggage in a store as I was under no illusions as to the amount of personal kit I could take into the Burma jungle. The next stage in my journey was another train journey from Calcutta to Chittagong. It was at the Chittagong Transit Camp that I got a taste of what was to come. The monsoon was on and the roof of my bamboo hut leaked and I had a miserable night.

Thank God I was not long to be in this 'hell hole' as arrangements had been made for me to journey through the jungle to join the 1 Sierra Leone Regiment at Lalaroa in the Kaladan Valley. I was to meet with Lieutenant F. A. N. Matthews (called Fanny in the Regiment where he was the Battalion Signals Officer). The party consisted of Matthews and myself and two Africans to carry our kit. My recollections of this journey from Chiringa are a little dim but I remember at least five days in a canoe on the Sangu River in spate with two Africans as pilots – absolutely terrifying!

The following days we bashed our way through on jungle paths and every evening just as we were organizing for the night the rain would come down and the leeches would become active. Fanny Matthews was a splendid companion and always did his best to raise my flagging spirits after the day's march.

About the third or fourth day's marching, we stopped the night with the 1 Gambia Regiment which was commanded by my old friend Tony

Read. His Battalion was in a delightful place on the banks of the Sangu River where the Battalion was resting. We had a riotous evening and an abundance of whisky. Tony gave me a lot of advice which was to be of enormous help later on. Two or three days later we reached Battalion H.Q. of 1 Sierra Leone Regiment at Lalaroa, 'Journey's End'. It had been an exhausting march for me particularly as I had been in an office with no physical exercise for many months previously.

However, I at least had the experience of a trek through dense bamboo jungle very similar to the campaign to follow. I had a warm welcome from my Commanding Officer, Colonel Kenneth Carter, who was to be a friend and counsellor during the weeks to follow. We were in a semi-operational area at Lalaroa, the Battalion Command Post was in a deep 'dug-out' covered by a bamboo roof and a tarpaulin and lit by hurricane lamps.

During those first days, I was taken round all the Companies and introduced to my brother officers and here I should say that I knew no-one in 1 Sierra Leone Regiment, had no experience of jungle fighting and had no knowledge of the Sierra Leone Africans. I cannot, after nearly fifty years, remember the names of *all* the Officers and British N.C.O.s but those with whom I had day-to-day dealings were Bill Dawkins (a Political Officer in the Gold Coast who was later to become my Second-in-Command), Francis Drake (the Battalion Adjutant), Peter Clements (the Intelligence Officer), Major Peter McArthur, Captain Hesketh and Lieutenant Philip Pitt. All these Officers had taken part in the first Kaladan campaign and were very experienced in jungle warfare which of course I was not, but later as Commanding Officer I was given enormous help and support from all my Officers.

The first few weeks as Second-in-Command with Ken Carter, the Commanding Officer, were taken up with visits to the outlying Companies and generally learning how to live in the jungle in the monsoon. I seem to remember that my sleeping arrangements were a bamboo bed with roof covered with two groundsheets and when it rained heavily I got wet!!

After about five weeks I was given the job of commanding a force of two Companies with orders to liquidate some Indian National Army known to be in the area and without fail to take prisoners. This operation was unsuccessful, we spent a whole day scouring the jungle with no result. At this stage I feel that I cannot do better than produce the story of 1 Sierra Leone Regiment, the Regiment I was fortunate to command in the operations known as 'Kaladan II' after the departure of Lt. Colonel Carter on long leave in mid-October.

Amongst my Wartime Memoranda I have in my possession a copy of the booklet *History of the 1st Bn. The Sierra Leone Regiment RWAFF 1939–1945*.

The content of this booklet is almost entirely devoted to the two campaigns Kaladan I and Kaladan II in the Burma Campaign of World War II – I was commanding the Battalion during the Kaladan II campaign and I have established from my Intelligence Officer at the time, Captain Peter Clements, that he was the main contributor to the story of these operations and is in agreement for it to be republished in my book.

As the Commanding Officer of the Battalion in Kaladan II, I believe it to be a full and accurate story of the events during this period of the Battalion's history.

After our return to Chiringa we reorganized and ran cadres for junior A.N.C.O.s. Our new General Maj.-Gen. Loftus-Tottenham, D.S.O., had taken over from Maj.-Gen. C. G. Woolner, C.B., M.C., who originally formed and trained the Division and led it through the first campaign. Maj.-Gen. F. Loftus-Tottenham, D.S.O., came to us during a difficult period with an inspiring record from the Gurkha Parachute Bde. He quickly gained the confidence of all ranks, and even the youngest private soldiers took the trouble to learn his name, the variations of which were both many and amusing.

He was destined to lead the Division to a triumphant conclusion of the Kaladan Campaign, and there is no doubt in the minds of all ranks that it was due to his personal leadership, utter contempt of danger and above all the Japanese, that enabled the Division to give the Jap such a thorough trouncing.

By the 12th August the Bn. was on the move again when 'C' Coy. left for the now familiar Sangu River en route Tanchi, where the rest of the Bde. was still concentrated. The Bn. followed and for more than two weeks in the midst of the heavy rains of the Arakanese monsoon, groups of the unit laboriously made their way up the swollen river. Progress was only possible by pulling the canoes with ropes (in the few cases where any kind of towpath existed) or more often tugging at the reeds of the river banks and so edging slowly upstream.

One recalls how many partly submerged reeds had hundreds of ants swarming to their tops, and these had to be pushed under-water before a handhold could be made.

The Battalion's orders were to concentrate at Singpa (taking over from a detachment of 4th N.R.). They were then to probe forward to contact the Japs and I.N.A. whom 4th N.R. patrols reported in Mowdok, three miles West of the India-Burma frontier, and Labawa, a village outpost on a commanding feature a mile North on our axis of advance.

Much of the patrolling was done in the very difficult and sometimes nearly impossible conditions of rain, muddy hill paths and flooded chaungs.

By the time our last troops had concentrated at Singpa, our forward Coy. in position on the high ground astride the track midway between the river and Lalaroa, had had several clashes with an enemy ambush forward of the ruined village. A few parties of mixed Japs and I.N.A. approached our strongly dug positions from various directions, but the enemy appeared content most of the time to sit and await our coming.

'B' Coy. occupied a position opposite the Jap ambush on 22nd Sept. A single A.O.R. (Pte. Shekku Koinadugu) on the same day sprang the enemy ambush. He had gone forward from our own ambush position with only a grenade as he had heard movement down the track. Having advanced about 100 yards he found himself in the centre of an enemy position. They opened fire wildly in all directions, but he dived down a steep bank and returned unharmed. We patrolled all round this strong enemy outpost, and inflicted several casualties in skirmishes. Air strikes were available and gave good support but on many occasions had to be called off owing to heavy rain. A platoon of 'B' Coy. eventually seized the position with mortar support, and the enemy withdrew to their main positions.

A series of difficult patrols was necessary to find the extent and dispositions of the enemy troops and to find ways round them, and a 'C' Coy. patrol (Capt. Curnow and C. S. M. Boulton) succeeded in cutting a track by-passing the Jap positions to the East.

After an airstrike, however, and mortar concentration from 102 Mortar Regt. Sgt. Smith's platoon of 'A' Coy. brushed forward up the main track and occupied the heavily bunkered defences without opposition. A quantity of Jap and I.N.A. equipment was found and the headcover of the Jap trenches was found to be fully effective against our mortar fire but accurate bombing by the R.A.F. scored several direct hits completely demolishing the positions.

The Jap appeared to have resorted to his old tactics and made a long withdrawal. Mowdowk was entered by Lieut. Woodham's platoon of 'A' Coy. on 8th Oct. 'D', 'C' and 'B' Coys being quickly built up there. Patrols however soon bumped Jap positions along the difficult track up to the frontier, and a series of attacks by fighting patrols was made to dislodge the Jap on either side.

Sgt. Bennett commanding a platoon of 'C' Coy. was heavily engaged in the area where 'A' Coy. had harboured whilst road making nine months previously. The Sgt. and Cpl. Ansumana Koranko pinpointed twelve enemy positions by crawling very close under fire. The A/Cpl. was awarded an immediate M.M. for his work here, throwing several grenades at point blank range into the enemy bunkers, and effectively covering his and Sgt.'s withdrawal with a phosphorus grenade. At this point he was so close that he himself received burns from the grenade as he withdrew with a bullet in the leg and neck.

'C' and 'B' Coys. and Tactical H.Q.s dug in 500 yards from the enemy with the leading 'C' Coy. platoon only 200 yards from the Jap bunkers.

The next four days was spent in heavy harassing fire by our Mortars and

L.M.G.'s, airstrikes, and attempts to by-pass his defences, which our frontal had proved to be very strong.

The final approach to these positions was up 200 yards of narrow slippery track and up a steep slope, and it seemed that heavy casualties would have to be accepted to drive the Jap back into Burma.

After an airstrike 'D' Coy. probed forward but were held up by heavy M.G. fire and mortars. Two very gallant A.O.R.s were killed when within only a few yards of the Jap bunkers. A very accurate bombing and strafing by our supporting Hurricanes enabled 'C' Coy. to occupy the enemy positions, and to get troops dug in 200 yards forward.

We lost our Commanding Officer, Lt. Col. K. P. M. Carter, M.C., here when he proceeded on long leave after nine months' continuous campaigning. His place was taken by Major P. T. van Straubenzee, who had joined us six weeks previously and had quickly settled down in spite of the most unpleasant conditions.

Major Dawkins (O.C. 'A' Coy.) rejoined us here from a staff course and took over 2 i./c.

A.O.R. patrols soon discovered that the Jap had more positions actually on the boundary line, 600 yards further East. Lieut. Edwards' platoon fought a sharp engagement against the enemy during the morning of the 18th Oct. That night produced a lively exchange of small arms and mortar harassing fire, and after an airstrike on the following morning Lieut. Pitt's platoon of 'C' Coy. found the enemy had had enough. That night in fact we had established two Coys' (u/c 2 i/c) in the Jap positions on the frontier.

These positions stretched several hundreds of yards on each side of the jeep road, heavily bunkered and wired with an extensive communicating trench system. The defences stretched to the highest point of the range two miles to our North, where 4th N.R. had experienced a similarly difficult time.

At the completion of this operation, the last Jap had been driven from Indian soil, and the Bde. received a message of congratulation from the Corps Commander.

The frantic haste of the Japanese withdrawal had been accelerated by the wide encircling move of the 5th Bde. It had cut the Kaladan River, the main Japanese L of C, several miles South of the jeep road after exploring and making a path over the frontier range through the most impossible country where no track had ever existed.

On the 18th Oct. Labawa, our Bn. H.Q. on our first arrival, was reported clear. 'A' Coy. exploited the following day to Laingthan, finding there a Jap harbour where the enemy's cooking fires were still burning.

The Bn. now had five days' rest, which was most welcome and gave the troops their first opportunity to swim and wash their clothes since leaving the Sangu six weeks before.

Our most able and tireless Quartermaster, Capt. (Q.M.) Sayers was evacuated sick while we were here. A lot of the credit for the fine morale of the troops throughout this long and arduous campaign must be given to Capt. Sayers' organization of our supplies. We were fortunate however that his

R.Q.M.S. (R.S.M. Bryanton) although waiting to go to his new unit as R.S.M. remained with us for the rest of the second campaign, and the complicated problems faced by a Bn. on air supply never gave us a moment's anxiety.

Supplies were always plentiful but in the first campaign there was a certain amount of monotony in the diet, and particularly no fresh meat, except occasional local purchase of airstrike-wounded beef. In the second phase, however, a great improvement was noticed, and there were plentiful supplies of fresh meat and rice for the A.O.R.s, while eggs and even live poultry were dropped by parachute.

It was while we were here that the Gambia Regt. passed through us and with the 4th N.R. left on frontier hill our task was to escort Bde. H.Q. and auxiliary troops in the advance down the Pi Chaung. The Bde. column moved swiftly South meeting no opposition, until during the first week of November the Gambia Regt. bumped strong enemy delaying positions in the Kru Chaung. With 4th N.R. still detached from the Bde., the Bn. had several 'odd jobs' to do mainly concerned with the placing of 'stoppers' on the more likely approaches to the flanks of our advance.

B' Coy. (u/c Capt. Davies, vice Major Green now on leave) spent two uneventful nights covering a track junction some miles East of the Bde. 'A' Coy. (u/c Major Brisco) were also detached on the West flank preventing Jap interference from track leading with the Pi Chaung from the S.-W.

The Coy. and its patrols were constantly in contact for the week that they were away. The enemy in small parties came around their positions from various directions, putting over harassing fire with M.G.s and Mortars and using 'jitter' tactics and catcalls.

While the 1st Gambia Regt. were steadily pushing back the enemy in the Kru Chaung, a Jap O.O. captured by 5th Bde. in the Paletwa area caused a change in the Divisional plan. The whole Bde. was ordered to concentrate at Auklo where 4th N.R. would join us.

There followed on 16th Nov. probably the most difficult march the Bn. had ever had to do, but nothing will ever compare with the rocky cliff face which dropped almost sheer from the summit of the mountain range overlooking the Kaladan valley. We admired probably our finest view of the river and the mountains far to the East, and then proceeded with hours of slipping and sliding and clambering down the precipitous descent. We had started off at dawn. Fifteen hours later bodies of troops from the column were still marching in to the Auklo harbour. No praise can be too high for the unarmed soldiers of the Aux. Group and our own Bn. who toted their heavy loads across this range throughout the heat of the day and well on into the night. The most amazing feat of all was the carry by 6th Fd. Ambulance of 16 stretcher cases safely down the cliff in the dark by the light of bamboo torch flares. Of the whole column only one missed his footing in the dark, and with his load was pulled up undamaged by means of a rope from a rocky chaung bed 20 feet below.

At Auklo the Bn. task was to seize the high ground to the East, to clear it as far as Paletwa and to dominate the river, while the remainder of the Division pushed South.

For several days the Bn. shared with the Jap the high ground overlooking our Divisional Moth strip. Daily airstrikes and continuous mortar harassing and infantry attacks failed to shift the Japanese from his very strong position. He was dug in on a pimple and effectively covered the only approach, a narrow knife-edged ridge.

On the 23rd Nov. after the second heavy airstrike of the day, a platoon of 'B' Coy. led by Lieut. Clements and Sgt. Johnson succeeded after a fierce battle in putting the gallant defenders to flight. The platoon went in shouting 'Sierra Leone' and many more epithets about the Jap pouring in a great volume of automatic fire and grenades, and finishing off with the bayonet the only Jap who had failed to make good his escape.

Another body was found in the position, several rifles and much equipment had been abandoned, and many graves were found later in the line of retreat. The enemy were identified as a squadron of our old friends 55th Cavalry for whose fighting qualities we already had the greatest respect.

The clearing of this position had cost us four A.O.R.s wounded.

A patrol of 'C' Coy. led by Lieut. Innes had meanwhile located a large force of Japs digging in on the hills between us and Paletwa. A quickly organized airstrike caught the enemy completely by surprise while he was hastily preparing his positions. Very heavy casualties were undoubtedly inflicted and the enemy moved in a panic across the river during the night. A few stragglers only remained and 'C' Coy. cleared the area and established themselves on the feature. Their clerk (L/Cpl. Joseph Yambasu) shot dead a straggler who was found wandering on the near bank.

The Bn.which was now alone in the area had the further task of observing the movements of the enemy force across the river. This necessitated the crossing of small recce patrols to the far bank. Capt. Mitchell crossed first and for 48 hours remained in observation sending back by wireless most valuable information. Lieut. White and Lieut. Clements also crossed in different places to the North and were able to report no movement in that direction.

Meanwhile Lieut. Pitt made a very hazardous crossing to a place where enemy sentries had been seen by Capt. Rose who had established standing patrols for observation purposes several days previously. Although separated from his small patrol, Lieut. Pitt remained in observation by himself for 36 hours and returned with the information that no large numbers of enemy were now in the area.

On Dec. 2nd we started the long march to rejoin the Bde. who successfully sweeping light enemy opposition before them, had made a wide encircling movement to the West and reached the Kaladan opposite Tinma.

We had been joined at Akulo by the 21st A/Tk. Regt. and marched with them for the first two days down the Pi Chaung. Order then came to the Bn. to move independently by forced march to the Kyingri loop then held by the 5th Bde. and 81 Recce Reg. After two days' hard marching on half rations we reached the loop and without a rest set off before daybreak to join the Bde. next day at Tinma West after fourteen more miles and two river crossings.

The Kyingri Dakota strip had been seized undamaged, and was used nonstop for three days. In this time 1,000 reinforcements for the Division were flown in and all casualties evacuated.

1st Gambia Regt. who had led the crossing of the Kaladan, formed a bridgehead without opposition, and quickly established themselves in Tinma East. The tail of a Jap column moving South had been seen and shot up by the leading Gambia Coy. and it was clear that the enemy were both bewildered and disorganized by the Division's rapid advance South.

On the evening of the 9th we were shelled for the first time, having one A.O.R. wounded. Jap artillery harassing fire at night became a regular occurrence from this date. The following day the Bde. joined Gambia in Tinma East and 5th Bde. took over the positions.

For the fortnight that we were here we had a comparatively quiet time, but a patrol led by Lieut. Strickland ('D' Coy.) soon established that all tracks leading South down the foothills were firmly blocked by the enemy. One A.O.R. was killed in this skirmish.

We found time to organize a game of cricket on the Moth strip at Tinma and one of the strangest matches ever was played to the accompaniment of mortars ranging round us, the distant sound of small arms fire, and continued interruptions by Moths taking off a few feet over our heads in a cloud of dust. Lt. Col. van Straubenzee's XI lost to Lt. Col. Charles Walwyn's XI by 48 runs, largely due to a fine innings of 88 by Lieut. Smith of 4th Aux. Group, Sierra Leone Regt.

The gods of war must have thought we were treating them too light-heartedly, for a few hours after stumps were drawn and flown out, a Jap counter-attack on 5th G.C.R. began and with heavy artillery fire continued until the next morning.

The Divisional plan was to deceive the enemy by demonstrating down the paddy (very successfully achieved by 5th Bde. who in so doing completely routed the powerful Jap counter-attack up the left bank of the river). 6th Bde. was at the same time to move over the hills round the enemy's right flank and establish itself behind the Jap's considerable main force round Kyauktaw.

1st Gambia Regt. and 4th N.R. patrols to Thandada over in the Yan Chaung found a way across the mountains and the Fd. Coys. quickly established a track and made it muleable in their own amazingly quick way.

The move to Thandada began on 18th Dec. with 1st Gambia Regt. in the lead and the Bn. brought up in rear of the Bde. column on the following day.

The Gambians quickly swept light Jap resistance before them and we reached Thandada area at midday on 21st after strenuous marching and a waterless first day. The same afternoon 'C' and 'D' Coys. with the C.O. and Tactical H.Q. moved up the steep track to a high ridge which overlooked both the Kaladan plain and the proposed Bde. box. 'C' Coy. seized our objective (the dominant feature point 887) and by dusk the small force was dug in astride the track without opposition.

The enemy's complete mystification caused by our rapid moves was shown just before daylight on the following morning.

A party of Japanese some 30 strong walked up the way we had come straight into our Tactical H.Q. The track was held by a powerful ambush of two sections of the A.A. platoon with riflemen from the mortar platoon on the track to the command post. The ambush opened up and four Japs including the Capt. i/c force came through it only to be shot dead at close quarters by L/Cpl. Bobo Jumbo and the other Mortar riflemen. The ambush completely broke up the remainder on the narrow path, and the panic-stricken Japs rushed in all directions, many falling down the steep hillside, and were systematically destroyed during the next hour.

The considerable slaughter of the enemy force was largely due to the A.A. Pl. Sgt., Ansana Beya who by striding up and down the position with a Bren gun himself accounted for at least six Japanese. As a result of this action he was awarded an immediate D.C.M.

A few Japs (including one carrying a wounded man on his back) broke down the path away from Tactical H.Q. and bolted through 'D' Coy. H.Q.: One was killed by a follower and the other by the Coy. Commander, Capt. Mitchell who could hardly have had time to disentangle himself from his mosquito net before getting his Sten gun into action.

In all, twelve Japanese bodies were recovered and one wounded prisoner of war who died in our A.D.S. later. The dead included the Capt. in command of the enemy and a signaller who blew himself and his wireless set up with a grenade.

A mass of equipment, an L.M.G. and two light mortars of a new pattern together with most valuable documents and marked maps were amongst the considerable booty.

Our very slight casualties included one A.O.R. killed and a splinter in the back of Lieut. Pitt, A.A. Pl. Commander from a grenade thrown by the leading Jap troops. The remainder of the Bn. less 'A' Coy. joined us later that morning.

'A' Coy. had been left to block a side track into the Yen Chaung. They were engaged in a small battle in which one platoon (Lieut. White) charged with war cries and put to flight a section of Japs dug in near the Coy. position. The Coy. rejoined the Bn. late that evening.

During the next 48 hours enemy artillery heavily engaged us by night and we had two patrol clashes by day. In one of these 'B' Coy. recovered a knee mortar, two rifles and bloodstained equipment. One A.O.R. was killed in this clash but no other casualties were suffered.

Christmas Day 1944 will be long remembered by the Bn. Two sections of Lieut. Strickland's platoon had a skirmish in the afternoon forward of the Bn. position and killed three Japs. Just before dark that evening the Japs opened up a fierce artillery bombardment into our area, the shells falling mainly into 'D' Coy. Bn. H.Q. and the 102 Mortar Battery.

The bombardment went on continuously for 25 minutes and was followed by two simultaneous attacks by a Jap Coy. who had moved up under cover of the shelling. One attack was directed against 'D' Coy. and the other against Lieut. Reade's platoon of 'C' Coy. covering 'Bn. H.Q. Very heavy M.G. and grenade fire assisted the enemy attack. Several knee mortar bombs landed in

Bn. H.Q. and one wounded Sgt. Winn (O.R.S.) in the stomach. Sporadic shelling added to the weight of the attack. One shell in fact pitched into the slit trench of Lieut. Strickland ('D' Coy.) who had left it a few seconds before to visit his section positions. He was fortunately untouched.

Our troops however were well dug in and our panji belt was by now 30 yards deep and as the enemy closed to the edge of this fence, so he was shot down by our L.M.G. fire. After two hours both attacks had been driven off, and although we suffered casualties, the enemy who had got close enough to start pulling out our panjis below 'D' Coy. must have suffered several times as many.

We lost four A.O.R.s killed, while Sgt. Winn and 17 A.O.R.s were wounded.

The enemy beaten, was still moving round in the bush, probably trying to find and evacuate his dead and wounded, and occasional sniping by our troops continued through the night.

A short intensive burst of enemy shelling started again in the early morning but all shells were well over our heads. The Bn. had come through the worst artillery bombardment it had yet known, and one of the fiercest infantry attacks. In spite of this the troops' good spirits never left them, and the Divisional Commander who visited us next morning at once noticed this and congratulated the Bn. on a good job of work.

For the rest of our stay on Pt. 887, patrolling was our chief concern mainly on to the paddy to the North and West. We did however get a magnificent view of the very heavy air bombardment of a Jap-held hill feature (Westdown) in the paddy. We saw 300 tons of bombs dropped by Mitchell bombers cause columns of black smoke from Jap ammunition dumps and stores to climb hundreds of feet in the air above the devastated enemy area.

It is significant of the Jap disorganization that, although we had fought a battle on 22nd Dec. fifteen miles in his rear and although the complete Division had moved to the Yan Chaung area by 21st Dec. yet the bewildered Jap made a fierce attack on our empty Divisional harbour at Tinma as late as 23rd Dec.

The Bn. advanced South on 29th Dec. with the 4th N.R. in the lead. No opposition was met until Angthaung where the Bde. concentrated. Here we again lost 'A' Coy. who went forward u/c 4th N.R. to thicken up the South end of the box. While detached, 'A' Coy. had a busy time. A platoon of Japs attacked by night Lieut. Campbell's platoon which was in an isolated position on the 4th N.R.'s left flank. The platoon effectively drove off the enemy, capturing a wounded prisoner of war and six rifles.

The main Bn. positions again came in for heavy shelling. Our only close contact, however, came in two patrol battles, and 'C' Coy. troops twice sent back small enemy recce parties with little information about our harbour to show for several casualties inflicted on them.

After two unpleasant nights of Xmas Rains the advance continued. 'A' Coy. of 1st Gambia Regt. was sent round the enemy's left flank across a wide chaung. They succeeded after a heavy Medium Bomber strike in establishing a bridgehead, and half the Bn. went through to seize the main feature (Starfish) without opposition.

The remainder of the Bn. harboured near a bridge constructed by the Sappers ready to build up the following day.

'D' Coy. and 'H.Q.' Coy. here were heavily shelled that night. Only two A.O.R.s were wounded, although a 'D' Coy. man actually received two direct hits on the log roof of his trench and was himself untouched.

The previous B.25 bombardment had thinned out the cover on Starfish and the enemy must have had a good idea of our dispositions. The remainder of the Bn. closed up on the feature on the morning of the 11th and a few hours after nightfall heavy shelling started from 105 mm and 75 mm guns and a heavy mortar. It continued until an hour before dawn and was later increased by a 70 mm Jap Bn. gun opening up from close range. Although we lost our night's rest, nobody at all was hit.

Our patrols located Japs a few hundred yards south of us down the spine of the ridge, and 'B' Coy. were pushed forward to contain them until 4th N.R. could pass through and continue the advance. On the morning of the 13th 'B' Coy. were caught by mortar fire as they were digging in and suffered some casualties (two A.O.R.s killed, and one attached R.E. officer and 12 A.O.R.s wounded). In addition six A.O.R.s were slightly wounded but remained in action. The enemy, however, was still content to wait for us and no close contact was made.

After six hours more shelling the next night, a 'B' Coy. party was taken forward by the Coy. Commander, Capt. Rose, early on the morning of the 15th Jan. to clear the next pimple prior to the 4th N.R. advance. The patrol, however, bumped two concealed L.M.G. posts and we lost a valuable and very gallant officer when Capt. Rose was killed at close range. Two unsuccessful attacks by the 4th N.R. showed that the opposition was strong and the axis of the Bde. advance was changed.

1st Gambia Regt. pushed S.E. and secured a base at Atetkwong-young. Our job when the Bde. moved on 20th Jan. was to pass through and secure the right bank of the Lemro River, twelve miles to the east.

Meanwhile 5th Bde. were making progress in spite of opposition down the foothills commanding the motor road and the gradual encirclement of the Divisional objective – the important Jap base of Myohaung now began.

The Bn. established itself on 21st without opposition at Poyogyi on a bend in the Lemro, although many signs of recent occupation were reported by our vanguard platoon (Lieut. Innes) of 'C' Coy. We did a sweep down the right bank of the river with the other two Bns. also pushing south in separate columns.

A platoon of 'A' Coy. (Lieut. Davey) was sent forward to secure an isolated pimple covering the river at Lenvindaung and had a hectic time. A little shelling round his positions during the night was followed by his successful dispersal of a Jap patrol on the morning that the Bn. came up behind him.

The same evening very accurate ranging shots were fired by the Jap gunners, and half an hour after midnight an intensive barrage was put down for a quarter of an hour. This was followed by a platoon attack with L.M.G.s, grenades and derisive shouts and it was three hours before the Jap finally gave up. Three A.O.R.s wounded were our only casualties in this determined defence. The platoon was withdrawn to the Bn. perimeter for the next night, and renewed Jap artillery harassing fire continued for some hours on to empty positions. The outpost was successfully reoccupied during daylight.

82 Recce Bn. passed over the River Lemro from our area to drive south down its left bank.

The Bn. led the Bde.'s final advance on 4th Jan. down a crooked route discovered by Capt. Evans' recce patrol from 'D' Coy. Previous patrol clashes had shown all known tracks to be held by rearguards of the Jap force which was desperately trying to evacuate their last troops and stores from Myohaung – now surrounded by eleven Battalions. We succeeded in reaching Pt. 404 (our last objective) dominating the paddy between Myohaung and the river in the early morning of 25th Jan. when a platoon of 'C' Coy. (Capt. Briscoe) slowly cut their way through the difficult but covered way along the hill tops.

We dug in for the last time and heard later that the Divisional Commander had ridden into Myohaung on a charger and taken the salute in a ceremonial march through the town.

On the 29th Jan. the Bn. marched out of active operations through the town and after concentrating at Westdown, started the eight days march to Buthidaung, and thence by lorry to Chiringa.

We were proud to learn a few days later of the awards of the M.C. to Major McArthur and Lieut. (now Capt.) White and the B.E.M. to R.S.M. Bokari Farandugu for distinguished service in the first campaign.

The Bn. had been engaged in Long Range penetration operations for thirteen months. They marched at a conservative estimate 1,000 miles. Patrols probably covered twice that distance. They soldiered in the jungle throughout the monsoon (except for five weeks in Chiringa) and had been in contact with the enemy practically the whole time.

For the ordinary rifleman, it meant over a year's daily digging, a year's marching as heavily laden as any troops in the world, a year's continuous sentry-go in country where no unit could ever consider itself 'in reserve'. A year of pitched battles, patrols and ambushes.

For the Europeans, the Platoon Commander, Subaltern or B/Sgt. great mental and nervous strain must be added to the normal responsibilities of leadership. Our Corps Commander's Order of the Day issued after the triumphant climax to our campaign in the capture of Myohaung pays tribute to what the S.E.A.C. newspaper called 'The Special Force of 15th Corps'.

After a short but well-earned rest the time came for the Battalion to move back into India.

'B' Coy. left on the night of 2nd March u/c Major Drake to carry out all baggage duties, etc., for the Bn. at Chittagong. The main body u/c Lt. Col. P.T. van Straubenzee was to move by road to Dohazri and by rail to Chittagong.

On the morning of the 3rd March, the Bn. was astir early and transport, 57 trucks in all, arrived at 05.00 hrs. to convey us to Dohazri. The scene was reminiscent of Piccadilly Circus as the trucks with headlights blazing circled the roundabout in the camp. Rolls were called as the troops embussed and at 06.00 hrs, the Bn. moved off from Chiringa, and as we went past the Guard

Room, the bugles of the Regimental Band sounded the farewell.

The Bn. entrained at Dohazri that evening and arrived at Chittagong to find a meal already prepared and three canteen cars where the troops were able to purchase plenty of cigarettes and food.

We embarked at 16.00 hrs. and troops were allocated their mess decks, the accommodation being very good. As the ship was not due to sail that night a football match was played ashore between the Officers and B.N.C.O.s versus the Ship's crew which resulted in a win for our team.

On board were many old friends, most of whom were proceeding on repatriation – Major Black of the 4th Nigeria Regt. was in charge of the party.

Others on board were Major Smibert, 6th Fd. Ambulance, B/C.S.M. Greatrex ex 'B' Coy., R.S.M. Shekko Fofana and the first repats from the Bn., including Sumura Koranko, M.M., L/Cpl. Thomasi Buedu, M.M., and Sgt. Faiera Kangama ex-Defence Pl.

We sailed on the 5th March and it was a very pleasant trip, the food was quite good and organized tournaments of Tug-of-War and Deck Quoits were played off. We arrived at the Port of Madras at 08.00 hrs. on the 9th March and disembarked at 14.00 hrs. The troops were given cigarettes, sweets and soap by the Madras welfare associations. The Bn. marched through the town to the transit camp where an enjoyable week-end was spent.

On the 12th March the transport arrived and conveyed the Bn. to Karvetnagar.

It was a very well organized move and everything went off without a hitch.

The camp was the best laid out one we had yet seen, but terribly hot with no outside amusement for the troops. This was a great disappointment to all ranks who had been out of touch with civilization for nearly eighteen months.

War and rumours of war were prolific, every African having his own idea as to what we were going to do and where we were to do it. The first step came on 27th April when the Bn., now part of the 34 Corps moved down to Bombay and joined the Combined Operations Training Centre for a month's intensive training.

The month proved to be the most interesting and enjoyable period in the history of the Battalion.

For the first time A.O.R.s worked with British Commandos, scrabbled up nets, hurled themselves out of landing craft and stormed up long sandy beaches through roaring breakers. Their keenness was infective and our own Europeans and Instructors alike found it a pleasure to work with them. Time was short, with training periods hard and long, but the Bn. came through with flying colours and most welcome praise from the training staff.

The course ended with a glorious ten days leave in Bombay and all ranks made the most of it.

The bearing and discipline of the Battalion left nothing to be desired and our stay in Bombay ended all too soon. The troops seldom missed an opportunity of using the words of command learnt on training. Every time a train, lorry or rickshaw drew up one would hear the order 'Out kedge, down doors, land', and so it goes on to this day.

Chapter 9

Kaladan: A Personal View

As the Commanding Officer of 1 Sierra Leone Regiment I want also to record my own feelings, worries, tribulations, etc., in those momentous days when we started to get the 'Nips' on the run.

I had, of course met my Brigade Commander, Brigadier A. A. Crook, soon after my arrival in the Battalion and some weeks later Major General Freddie Loftus Tottenham, my Divisional Commander.

I had learned from them before the operations started in the Kaladan Valley that both expected aggressive action in future operations against the Japs.

We started operations in mid-October 1944 with the object of seizing Frontier Hill from the Japs, this being the scene of heavy fighting in the earlier campaign. I was still Second-in-Command but on October 18th when Lieutenant-Colonel Ken Carter left for leave after a long period in command, I took over command of the Battalion. In retrospect, I remember feeling somewhat diffident as to whether I could lead 1 Sierra Leone Regiment in a second campaign and retain the confidence and loyalty of my Officers, British N.C.O.s and Africans.

I had less experience than anyone in the Battalion of jungle fighting and consequently depended heavily on my H.Q. Staff – Bill Dawkins, my Second-in-Command, Francis Drake, my Adjutant, Jim Sayers, my Quarter Master and my Intelligence Officer, Peter Clements.

This quartet had the considerable experience of the first campaign and were always available for wise counsels. It was only a few hours after taking over command that the Battalion became involved in battle.

The night of October 18th was made hideous by rifle, light machine gun and mortar fire and both the Divisional Commander and the Brigade Commander demanded to speak to me on the No. 18 wireless set, clamouring to know the situation.

I was able to reassure them saying that I thought much of the firing was our own and that there was no cause for worry. The next morning Frontier Hill was ours.

As can be seen from the foregoing story, we pushed the Jap back relentlessly and it was an endless procession of daily marches through dense bamboo jungle. On many occasions the Africans had to cut a passage through the undergrowth with their machetes.

Throughout this campaign our rations were always supplied from the air and normal procedure was to have an air drop every third day, eating one day's rations and carrying the other two days' food with us on the march. Preparation for receiving an air drop from Dakota aircraft involved the selection and clearance of quite a large area of the jungle which was carried out by the Africans with their machetes. It was always exciting to see those lovely silk parachutes floating down and all in a variety of colours and I was able to keep a red and a yellow one and these were popular gifts to girlfriends.

Map reading was a nightmare to me – I was always a poor performer at it and my Intelligence Officer Peter Clements made the unforgettable remark, 'That the Commanding Officer is all right but only if he is pointed in the right direction''.

A picture of the dense Bamboo Jungle through which the Battalion was operating in the Kaladan Valley is included in the illustrations and the description of the march, which started on November 16th and previously referred to earlier in the story, is in no way exaggerated and we were all totally exhausted at the end of it.

Throughout this pursuit of the Japs, active patrolling continued night and day. Patrols commanded by a Subaltern Officer and a few Africans was a pretty unpleasant chore and a frightful strain on those concerned both physically and mentally. The jungle at night was particularly 'spooky' and frightening – one constantly heard noises as if hordes of 'Nips' were pushing their way through the dense undergrowth to attack us. But one of the main attributes of the African soldier was his ability to distinguish between the noise made by 'mortal man', i.e. Jap and other noises, i.e. animals.

Food supplies were pretty good but I remember one occasion when we were short – I woke up at about 2.00 a.m. one night and I was ravenously hungry. I crept stealthily to our mess kitchen, unseen I thought – not so, for there was the African cook protecting the meagre supplies – 'Commanding Officer Teefe Man' (thief). I was never allowed to forget it!

Sometimes, the bamboo was useful. The Jap had a nasty habit of creeping up to our Battalion perimeter defences at night to attack us. To discourage this Jap nastiness, we constructed 'pangies'. These were lengths of bamboo two to three feet in length with a sharp pointed end. These 'pangies' were stuck in the ground at an angle of forty-five degrees and pointing outwards towards any Jap threat and proved a deterrent for, besides causing pain, bamboo is also poisonous. The African troops carried a bundle of these 'obstructions' on their backs when moving to a new location. The bamboo was useful in other ways, our African orderlies used to knock up beds, tables, etc., very quickly and on the rare occasions when we had a day or two rest and were unlikely to be disturbed by the Japs, we would light fires for cooking (made of bamboo) which were smokeless and therefore permissible not giving away our harbour position to the Japs.

I well remember the operation mentioned on page 70 (November 23rd). This was a really unpleasant situation and I as the Commanding Officer was under extreme pressure from both the Divisional and Brigade Commanders to liquidate the Japs and seize the pimple. I refused to be hurried. Lives were at stake and I had strong words with high authority.

It would seem right to say here that throughout this campaign except for this incident my relations with my immediate Commanders was excellent and both Brigadier Crook (Crooky) and General Fred Loftus-Tottenham were always helpful and appreciative and both were 'front line' Officers and on many occasions came up to the 'sharp end' when there was a battle brewing.

Brigadier Crook's (Crooky) Operation Orders were always clear, simple and commendably brief and we three Commanding Officers seldom had to ask him for clarification at the end of an 'O' group. He almost always finished by giving us information on what support we might expect from our R.A.F. Fighter Bombers. The dialogue invariably went rather like this: 'Now, Philip, I know that you are being held up by the Japs on . . . feature. I will arrange for the Brylcreme Boys (Crooky's term of endearment for the R.A.F.) to plaster it and you must liaise direct with the Aircraft time of strike and indicate your target with coloured mortar flares.'

This cooperation with the R.A.F. worked tremendously well throughout the campaign and I recall the terrific bombardment the R.A.F. produced on my first operation (Frontier Hill) clearly greatly assisting us in our successful attack and later on many occasions my Battalion received enormous support.

On page 71 is an account of the cricket match played on the Tinma Moth strip on September 9th; it is in no way exaggerated and despite the Jap mortar fire great enjoyment was had by all. The newspaper *S.E.A.C.*, the mouthpiece of South-East Asia Command, had this to say:

Plymouth Ho Department

'Twenty-two British Officers and men of a Brigade of the 81st (West African) Division played cricket on a Kaladan Airstrip while Japanese guns and mortars shelled the area.

Two Lieutenant-Colonels challenged each other. The strip was dubbed the 'Kaladan Lords'. A message wirelessed for bats, balls, stumps and pads to be flown in at once and by two in the afternoon the game was on – fielders and batsmen clad in Jungle green.'

Gun and mortar fire continued intermittently throughout the game – British and Africans were spectators. It is an interesting fact that after that historic game of cricket, the Battalion was ordered to move at very short notice. That march of seventeen miles over narrow jungle paths, sometimes so steep that our sappers had to cut steps and always in drenching rain, was horrific and unforgettable.

The following night we heard that the Japs had mounted a full-scale attack on our empty cricket ground. This was surely a classic example of very good deception!

Our advance South proceeded to the Thandada area and the hair-raising and exciting incidents which occurred on Point 887 Thandada on December 22nd in pitch darkness is described on pages 71–3. It was a chaotic night and everyone with a weapon fired it. The noise was deafening, Lance Corporal Bobo Jumbo protecting my command post shot the Nip Officer and gave me the Jap Officer's sword which I took home to Spennithorne. Many years later my late wife, Imogen, suggested that since Bobo Jumbo probably saved my life the sword should be sent back to him in Sierra Leone. I agreed, and negotiations with the Colonial

Office in London were satisfactorily arranged and the sword was despatched to Sierra Leone. The sword was ceremoniously presented to Bobo in Freetown and the following account of what I understand to have been a colourful occasion was given in the *Sierra Leone Daily Mail* of August 23, 1965:

JAPANESE SWORD FOR SIERRA LEONE EX-SERVICEMEN'S ASSOCIATION

A Japanese sword captured by a Sierra Leone soldier, Lance Corporal, Bobo Jumbo of Blama in Burma in the Second World War will be presented to the SLESA, this week.

The presentation will be made by the Prime Minister, Sir Albert Margai in his capacity as Minister of Defence at a dance organised by the SLESA which will be held at the British Council Hall on Friday.

Lance Corporal Jumbo, who was in command of a section of the battalion Headquarters Defence Platoon in 1944, shot and killed a Japanese Commander who penetrated his battalion's position in their headquarters.

By this gallant act, Lance Corporal Jumbo saved not only his life but also that of his commander.

The Japanese sword was handed over by Lieutenant Colonel Philip van Straubenzee, who was in command of the battalion, to Lance Corporal Bobo Jumbo through the 81st West African (Division Club).

In a letter requesting the Prime Minister to make the presentation on his behalf, Lieutenant-Colonel van Straubenzee among other things stated 'would you, on my behalf, convey to Lance Corporal Bobo Jumbo my best wishes for his health and happiness in the future, and may this sword both serve as a constant reminder of the days that we fought side by side, and also inspire members of the SLESA to speed the completion of their new headquarters'.

The sword which arrived sometime last week, has been shown to the Prime Minister by the Secretary General of the SLESA, Alhaji Magba Kamara.

Lance Corporal Bobo Jumbo and ex-Regimental Sergeant Major Bockari Farandugu of Sierra Leone who served with the first Battalion throughout its two campaigns in Burma and ex-Company Sergeant Major Hassana Beya, the only Sierra Leonean who won the Distinguished Conduct Medal for gallantry in the field and Corporal Mamudu Samura, who was mentioned in despatches, will be presented at the dance.

The Acting Governor-General, Sir Samuel Bankole Jones, will also be present at the dance, which is in aid of SLESA's scholarship fund.

A picture of Lance Corporal Bobo Jumbo is included in the illustrations.

Our stay on Point 887 was quite a long one and the account of the Jap attack on Christmas night of 1944 is well told on pages 72–3. It is firmly imprinted on my memory, however, that we were extremely well 'dug in' with 'pangies' covering the whole Battalion position. It was pitch dark and everyone knew the only action was to stand firm and shoot when necessary and this is what we did. The attack was repelled.

In the brief peaceful period during that fortnight my eye caught a small paragraph in the financial column of a London newspaper. It was a 'tip' to buy some shares in Butlin's Holiday Camps as, the paper rightly predicted, 'Everyone would want a holiday when the war was over'. I invested a modest sum and forgot about it. When I reached home some eighteen months later, I found a very pleasant surprise. I had made a very profitable investment and this was the forerunner of other successful financial speculations when the War was over in 1946.

It was some time towards the end of the Kaladan Campaign that I had another minor difference of opinion with Brigadier Crook (Crooky). He used to ring me up late at night with orders for me to put down mortar harassing fire on the Jap positions. We all knew that what that meant was that the Japs would without fail return this fire in good measure. I formed up to 'Crooky' and complained bitterly and the nightly 'Jap hate' was abolished forthwith. He agreed for us to stop the evening Jap strafe. We all liked our tot of rum and especially 'Crooky' and this may have caused his enthusiasm for 'Nip hating' late at night.

The Kaladan Valley was a fantastically beautiful stretch of country and from our pinnacle on Point 887, the view of the river and the paddy fields had to be seen to be believed. 1 Sierra Leone Regiment was on its own at this time with higher authority many miles away.

I devised a pretty 'hare-brained' project that we should build rafts (with suitable protection) and paddle down the Kaladan River instead of the eternal march through the jungle. I still have the rough plan and sketch map for this enterprise which for some reason was not carried out.

It was early in January 1945 that I was called to Divisional H.Q. together with the Brigade Commander and Charles Walwyn the Commanding Officer of the 4th Nigerian Regiment. The reason for this summons was that Supremo, Lord Louis Mountbatten, had made a flying visit and wished to be introduced to the Senior Commanders of 6 West African Brigade, Royal West African Frontier Force.

This was a memorable occasion. He was extremely complimentary on the very successful operations carried out by 81 West African Division Royal West African Frontier Force during the previous months.

We continued to move South to join the Brigade, marching, patrolling and skirmishing until January 29th, 1945, when operations ceased. I have nothing to add to the story accurately told on page 70 onwards.

As Commanding Officer of 1 Sierra Leone Regiment during these strenuous and exciting days I was proud to have been chosen to lead the Battalion. I was inexperienced in jungle warfare whereas every other Officer, British N.C.O. and African other ranks had already completed an arduous campaign. I had to be taught and I had most loyal and cooperative support.

I cannot obviously mention everyone by name but Major Bill Dawkins, my second-in-command was an outstanding leader - Francis Drake my Adjutant, absolutely imperturbable in all circumstances (like I suppose his great namesake), Peter Clements, my Information Officer - indispensible - his map reading never failed! Major Peter McArthur, M.C., a most gallant and outstanding Company Commander, Captain Philip Pitt - I called upon him to undertake most unpleasant and dangerous patrols and frequently to cross the Kaladan River with Japs on the far bank. Captain and Quartermaster Jim Sayers - a most efficient and hardworking Quartermaster evacuated because of overwork and ill-health. Father Gannon, our Battalion Roman Catholic Priest was a close friend and administered faithfully to all denominations. Of our African Troops, Regimental Sergeant Major Bokari Farandugu was an outstanding character by any standard. It was he who organized the dug-outs at every battalion harbour area. He was greatly respected by all our British Officers and British N.C.O.s and the African Rank and File - his British Empire Medal was well deserved.

After a week or two at our camp at Karvetnagar, I was granted a fortnight's leave and I decided to go to Ceylon (Kandy) where I had had such an enjoyable tour of duty before the Kaladan Campaign. I was extremely fortunate to obtain a seat on a Dakota also taking Lady Mountbatten to Ceylon.

I had many friends in Kandy but I realized soon that Audrey was no longer interested in me which at the time was a disappointment - rather regretfully I gave her the yellow silk parachute!

It was, I believe, after about a week of my leave that I received a signal to return immediately and report to Divisional H.Q. I had no knowledge of what this recall from leave meant and made arrangements for my journey back to India as soon as transport was available. My only recollection of that journey (by train all the way) was of a foreboding of troubles ahead.

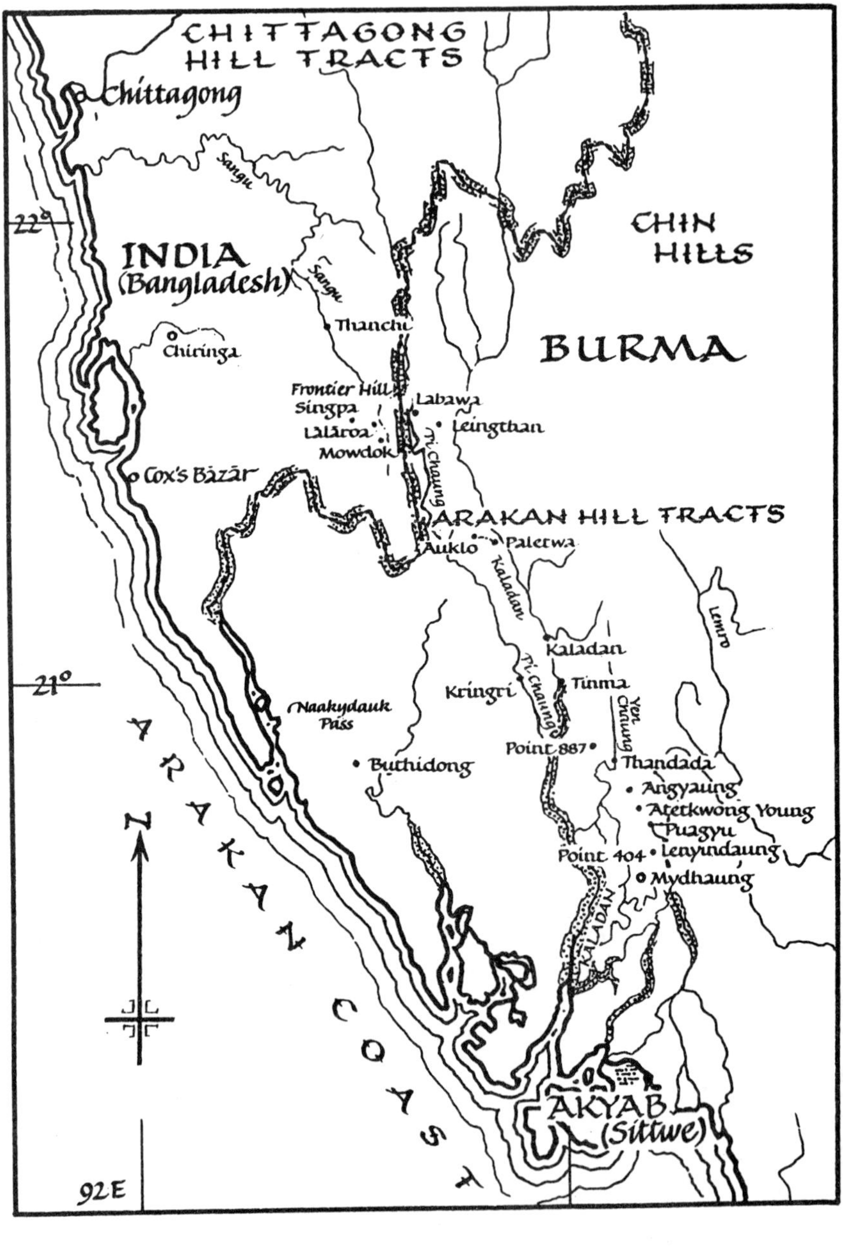
CHITTAGONG HILL TRACTS
Chittagong
Sangu
22°
INDIA (Bangladesh)
CHIN HILLS
BURMA
Thanchi
Chiringa
Frontier Hill
Singpa
Lalaroa
Mowdok
Labawa
Leingthan
Ti Chaung
Cox's Bazar
ARAKAN HILL TRACTS
Auklo
Paletwa
Kaladan
Lemro
21°
Kringri
Tinma
Yen Chaung
Naakydauk Pass
Point 887
Thandada
Buthidong
Angyaung
Atetkwong Young
Puagyu
Point 404
Lenyindaung
Mydhaung
ARAKAN COAST
AKYAB (Sittwe)
92E

Family homes at Spennithorne from a water colour painting by Lynne Moore.

General Sir Charles van Straubenzee and staff when commanding a brigade in the Crimea, 1854.

The looting of the Sebastopol Cross during the Crimean War, 1854. The cross now stands on the family vault at Spennithorne.

*My grandfather, Major General Turner van Strubenzee with left,
my brother Henry, and right, myself, at Spennithorne 1916*

The author when a corporal at Sandhurst

African safari, 1936 – a hazardous crossing.

My late wife, Imogen,

My daughter, Henrietta.

My daughter, Joanna.

My brother, Lieutenant-Colonel Henry van Straubenzee, D.S.O., O.B.E., when commanding the 4th/7th Royal Dragoon Guards.

General Sir Anthony Read, G.C.B., C.B.E., D.S.O., M.C.

Myself and Imogen being presented to Her Majesty the Queen on the occasion of a guard of honour for her from the 4th Battalion, the Green Howards (T.A.) at Teesside in 1955.

My nephew, then senior under officer Alexander van Straubenzee, being presented with the sword of Honour at Sandhurst by the late H. M. King Olav V of Norway, K.G. K.T. G.C.B., G.C.V.O., July 1971

Shooting party, Skelton Moor, Marske, 1989. From left to right, the author, Angela (my sister-in-law), Bill Fife, Henry van Straubenzee, William van Straubenzee.

My son-in-law, Nicholas

My father-in-law, Major General Walter Clutterbuck with left, nephew William, and right, nephew Charlie

My grandchildren — from left to right: Edward, Freddie and Victoria

My younger son-in-law, Gerry Farrell, 1983.

Self, Jeremy Graham, Sheilah Pitman, Tommy Pitman, Madeira, 1988.

Helen Wrightson and self, August 1989.

Skelton Moor, Marske. Lunchtime group of guns and guests on August 12th, 1989, on the occasion of the twenty-fifth anniversary of a partnership between the author and his landlords, William Allison Esq. of Telfit and Terry Allison Esq. of Moorhouse.

The Green Howards, tercentenary celebrations, 1989 – the author being presented to the Colonel in Chief, the late H.M. King Olav V of Norway, K.G., K.T., G.C.B., G.C.V.O., with General Sir Peter Inge, K.C.B., A.D.C. in attendance.

Chapter 10

Last Years as a Regular Officer

I was met at the station (name forgotten) by the G.S.O.I. of 81 West African Division Lieutenant-Colonel Alan Boggis, an old friend of many years standing. Alan told me that my period in command of 1 Sierra Leone Regiment was over and I would probably drop rank and get a staff appointment somewhere in India. He could not have been kinder or nicer and it must have been a difficult assignment for him to put over.

There was a guest night at Divisional H.Q. that same evening and I was to sit next to the principal guest who I think was General Sir Oliver Leese (the new Army Commander). I was too preoccupied with my own thoughts to make much conversation that night and I was to see General Fred Loftus Tottenham the next morning.

General Fred was a friend and I think he found that confrontation with me as difficult as I did. I cannot remember the full circumstances of my dismissal from Command of 1 Sierra Leone Regiment but 'loss of confidence in me' I believe was mentioned. It was, however, a shattering blow to me, particularly as I had just completed a successful campaign in the Burma jungles. At the end, when bidding me goodbye, General Fred said, 'I've recommended you for a D.S.O., you deserve it and I hope you get it.' I asked the advice of two of my greatest friends who had been with me in both campaigns, Tony Read and Pat Hughes, as to whether I should appeal against this decision but they both advised against it, and I am sure they were right. You seldom win a battle against Higher Authority!

It was all quite beyond me – it was a bitter blow and one that I was unable to forget for many months afterwards. After all these years, I still reflect as to the real reason why I lost command of 1 Sierra Leone Regiment in such a cavalier fashion and after the Kaladan Campaign was over. My Senior Commanders are no longer alive so it is probable that my dilemma will never be resolved.

The next day, I said my goodbyes to my many friends in 81 Division and my Battalion and was told that I could go on an indefinite period of leave until Higher Authority decided what to do with me.

I decided to go again to Arranmore, Lady Stow's leave camp at Outacummund where I had so enjoyed my last leave before going into Burma. I got a rapturous welcome from Lady Stow whose niece Ann Rennie, an Officer in the A.T.S., was also having some leave at Arranmore.

Ann was a very attractive girl and I fell for her in a big way. She was a good golfer and we played together on Outy's lovely course almost every day.

Time passed and I was unsettled. I had asked General Fred before I left the Division if he would recommend that I should be repatriated to the U.K. - I'm sure he did his best but with no avail and I was asked where I would like to go in a staff appointment in India. Ann Rennie, who had been a constant companion during the weeks of my leave, was stationed in Southern India (I forget where), and I asked if I could go there.

This posting also did not work out and I was instructed to report to G.H.Q. India in New Delhi where a job would be found for me. Once again the dreary, sweltering hot journey from Southern India to Delhi and my mood was anything but contented and I was totally disillusioned with my present unhappy circumstances. I had reached an all-time low by the time I had reached Delhi at past midnight. I had no verbal or written orders as to where to report so I stayed the night in the train which luckily had reached its final destination.

I duly reported at the Officers' Posting Branch (Military Secretary's Branch G.H.Q.) the next day. No-one knew anything about me but after hurried consultations I was given a Grade II appointment in the Military Secretary's Branch (Officers' Postings).

I spent a few days in one of the rather dreary Officers' Messes in New Delhi and then fortune smiled on me once again and someone (I can't remember who) recommended that in addition to my job at G.H.Q. Military Secretary's Branch, that I look after the Viceroy's Leave Camp in the Grounds of Viceroy's House. This was absolutely splendid news. I had the most beautiful and luxurious room in a lodge near the Viceroy's House and a bearer called Mukta. There will never be anyone like Mukta again, he would stand holding my trousers for me to step into! He would bring my dinner to my room if I decided not to go into the Leave Camp Mess.

My work at G.H.Q. Military Secretary's Branch Officers' Posting was by no means arduous and my staff consisted of a Staff Captain (name forgotten) but extremely nice – a Chief Clerk, Regimental Sergeant Major W. Smalley, very efficient and with whom I got on very well, and an extremely pretty Ceylonese girl called Dulcie – I was mesmerized by Dulcie and as she sat and worked in my office I found myself gazing at her for long periods.

My bosses were Colonel Shacklock and Lieutenant-Colonel Sam Key. They were both old and only turned difficult when Officers' postings went wrong and I was held to blame.

There were many advantages from being in a Viceregal Lodge and I soon became acquainted with many on Lord Wavell's staff, Colin Mackenzie and Bruce Fortune, Aide-de-Camp to Lord Wavell, Joanie, Lord Wavell's daughter (now Lady Joan Robertson), Lady Ann Fitzroy (now Lady Ann Mackenzie). Others not on the Viceroy's staff were Lieutenant-Colonel Eric Cooper Key, Major Harry Gordon, Lieutenant-Colonel Peter Fleming and Philip Mason and Major Nigel Noble. Many of these have been lasting friendships.

One incident which sticks in my memory whilst I was in Delhi was a flight to Southern India to deal with the posting of a large number of Officers who had arrived from the U.K. We left the Airport in a Dakota in fine weather but after about four hours ran into a really horrific tropical storm. There was thunder, lightning and torrential rain. I, with many other passengers, was violently sick and the pilot who was a wise man turned back to Delhi and we lived to go again three days later.

During my time in Viceregal Lodge New Delhi, Gerald Leet, a friend and an artist of considerable talent, asked if he might paint my portrait as a means for him to get some practice before embarking on the career he intended to follow when released from the Army.

It is my recollection that I was a troublesome and tiresome 'sitter' and that we had frequent squabbles and on one occasion I recall that in desperation he threw paint brushes at me. Needless to say, the portrait was completed and to this day hangs in the library at Spennithorne amongst the other family portraits where it was admired by all except my mother, now no longer alive, who complained that it gave me a 'discontented' look and she may well have been right! I believe that Gerald Leet had considerable success as a painter after the War and, I believe, became Art Master at Eton College.

It was at this time that Ann Rennie appeared on the scene once again having had a posting from Southern India to Delhi. We started again where we had left off in Outy and I became very attached to her. However, the atomic bomb had been dropped on Japan, the war was over and I wanted to go home. We decided to meet again in London at some future date.

I had great trouble in persuading the Authorities that I had a good case for repatriation to U.K. and only achieved it by asking my M.P. for Richmond, the late Captain Tommy Dugdale (Lord Craythorne), to produce a case strong enough to get me home. This he did for me and he has my lasting gratitude.

It was about halfway through my tour in Delhi that I learnt that I had been awarded a D.S.O. It came as a very great surprise to me as I felt that whatever General Fred had said the award would have been blocked after my downfall described earlier in this story. Anyway, this was a great boost to my morale especially as my brother Henry had also received a D.S.O. for his part in the Italian campaign.

The last few weeks in Delhi were taken in selecting and purchasing an Indian carpet of a size to fit the large Spennithorne dining room. There were literally hundreds of carpets of the correct size and I selected one – an inspired choice, I thought, which lies in the Spennithorne dining room to this day – 24 ft × 16 ft, its beautiful designs and colours exactly as it left the Delhi store forty seven years ago! Getting this carpet home to the U.K. was very exciting. Ten Indian bearers had to carry this carpet from the Calcutta Railway Station to the docks (Calcutta at this time was plagued with serious rioting) and then I had to persuade the Captain of the Troopship to agree to take it.

All was satisfactorily agreed and my crowning success was to persuade the U.K. Customs that this was in fact a secondhand carpet covering the floor of my mansion in Delhi. No duty was payable.

The voyage home was uneventful except for my meeting with the late Lieutenant-Colonel Freddie Spencer Chapman who was travelling back to the U.K. with his new wife Faith. He had had an adventurous War in the Malayan jungles in the Clandestine Force 136 and we were to share many Wartime experiences of life in these inhospitable places. He was later to write the account of his adventure in the best selling book *The Jungle is Neutral*. He had also been on one of the Everest Expeditions in the 1930s.

I had a long leave at Spennithorne – no great change in the way of life, in fact much the same as wartime with food and petrol rationing still in force.

The War Office Military Secretary's Branch asked me what I wanted to do – I said the War Office in some Branch of my choice. The first two offers were totally unacceptable to me, mainly dealing with manpower figures and mathematics, both subjects way beyond me.

I finally chose the Prisoner of War Directorate located in Northumberland Avenue. My task was the selection and general administration of the British Staffs in the Prisoner of War Camps in the U.K. of which there were upwards of about 180.

It was like a jigsaw puzzle fitting Officers into suitable slots. The telephone rang ceaselessly but I had a hardworking and competent staff – a Staff Captain, Captain Geoffrey Caterall, who mainly dealt with interpreters, a very efficient and charming secretary called Sheila Catherall who helped me through my early days in the job.

I hardly ever had any dealings with the Director Prisoners of War (D.P.W.), or with my immediate boss, a Colonel whose name escapes me.

I call to mind only one incident which possibly merits a mention. Brigadier A. A. Crook (Crooky) now reduced in rank to Lieutenant-Colonel visited me for the possible selection for command of a Prisoner of War Camp. I was at that stage 'all powerful' and could have sent him anywhere. I was, however, kind, and fixed him where he wanted to go. Whatever his failings, he was a fine front-line fighting Brigadier and I am glad he finished his days in a 'Grace and Favour' house at Windsor.

Those early days in London after the War were great fun. I was rather on the old side to be a 'Debs' Delight' but I was nevertheless invited to a fair number of dances. On one occasion at Claridges when the Queen (then Princess Elizabeth) was present, with rather too much champagne, I collapsed into the band with my unfortunate partner and all proceedings stopped whilst we picked ourselves up.

It was at this time the Ann Rennie arrived at home from India and we met on several occasions but it was not the same relationship that we enjoyed so much in India and we drifted apart though her Aunt, Lady

Stow, did her best to bring us together – she was a very attractive girl and I might have married her.

I invariably left London on Fridays for weekends at Spennithorne or to my brother Henry and my sister-in-law, Angela's, lovely home Kingscote in Berkshire. In the first few years after the War Henry and I rented a small grouse moor at Thornton Rust in Upper Wensleydale. This gave us enormous fun although birds were scarce.

It was in 1947 that with Henry we received an invitation to an honours ceremony at Buckingham Palace for our D.S.O.s to be presented to us by King George VI. This was an unforgettable occasion and my mother and sister-in-law, Angela, accompanied us.

My time at the War Office P. W. Directorate came to an end in 1948 and I was selected as Chief Instructor 3″ Mortars at the Small Arms School Netheravon.

A great friend, Colonel Sam Enderby, was the Commandant and the directing staff consisted of a further six Officers. The N.C.O. Instructors were all from the Small Arms School Corps – the Elite Weapons Instructors in the British Army.

The school possessed a fine partridge shoot and every Saturday in the season we used to walk up the birds on the lovely Wiltshire Downs. In Summer we were able to field a goodish cricket side and played most Saturdays.

I made some great friends at Netheravon; in addition to Colonel Sam Enderby, the Commandant, I remember Captain Ronnie Hedley Dent (The Deadly Hent) Adjutant; Major James Gresham, Irish Guards; Major Evans, the Machine Gun Instructor, and Colonel Stumps Green, Middlesex Regiment.

Sadly, after about eighteen months huge economies were being made in the armed forces and the Small Arms School at Netheravon came to an end and was disbanded. My 3″ Mortar Course was transferred to the School of Infantry at Warminster.

I now lived in a huge impersonal Officers' Mess amongst a large number of Officers unknown to me and I greatly missed the small and select happy family enjoyed at Netheravon.

Brigadier Mike West (later, the late General Sir Michael West), an old friend who served with me in the 43rd Infantry, was the Commandant of the School and I much enjoyed the hospitality of himself and his attractive wife Christine. Also, the late Brigadier Cecil Firbank (later Major General) became a close friend.

After about a year as Chief Instructor 3″ Mortars, a decision was made to restart the Support Weapons Wing and I as the Senior Weapons Instructor was called upon to organize its formation. Syrencot Manor was chosen as the new headquarters, a very attractive old country house not far from Netheravon.

I became the Acting Commandant of this New Weapons Wing with instructions to prepare for student's courses in 3″ Mortars, Anti-Tank Guns and Machine Guns with in addition the administrative problems of living quarters and feeding for staff and of course programmes for courses.

I much enjoyed this period in my life but realized that I was only an acting rank (Lieutenant-Colonel) and that a more Senior Officer would be selected to take over.

Brigadier Cecil Firbank who was then my boss asked me what I wanted to do when my successor arrived. I said I would like to return to the War Office where I had a luxurious flat in Cranmer Court, Chelsea, and in addition a lot of friends in London.

In 1950, I was appointed a Deputy Assistant Adjutant General in the Family Passages Branch of the War Office in Lansdown House and I was responsible for reunification of families who had got separated during the War years. This was a more difficult job than at first sounding and I found that in many cases husbands, who were being offered passages home to join their wives and families, preferred to stay abroad with, presumably, a girl friend. It was the same the other way round and sometimes wives did not wish to join their husbands abroad. Visits to see me in Lansdown House by a wife or husband were very often tricky and needed a great deal of tact.

I was extremely fortunate to have a Staff Captain called Mary Fforde. Mary was highly efficient and very charming. We got on well together and I always passed the difficult cases over to her for a solution.

I had a very attractive girlfriend at this time, her name was Venetia Bottril, she was divorced and was working in MI5. We used to have a sandwich lunch together in Green Park and on many occasions dined and danced together in the West End.

My bosses were Major General Sixsmith and a Colonel whose name I have forgotten but they never bothered Mary or myself.

For weekends I almost always stayed with my brother Henry and my sister-in-law Angela and almost always we played cricket for Bill Brakespeare's side at Henley. These were tremendously enjoyable weekends and I had many friends. We still rented Thornton Rust Moor in North Yorkshire so at weekends in August and September we would go up to Spennithorne for the grouse shooting.

Another old friend from wartime days in Ceylon, Gerry Waites, used to meet me at Lords and watch the cricket. Gerry fixed a meeting for me with Audrey Oliver, the Wren girlfriend I had in Ceylon, and for a short period we enjoyed ourselves in London's night life.

Unfortunately, after one and a half years the powers that be decided that I had spent long enough in 'Family Passages' and I was to be promoted to Lieutenant-Colonel and head a military mission in Saudi Arabia. I was absolutely horrified and the last thing I wanted was another tour of duty in a very hot climate where white women were very scarce!

I had no wish for promotion and only wanted the quiet peaceful existence of the last two years. I fought like a tiger to get my posting quashed but it was not easy as there were some Senior Officers in Military Secretary's Branch who were determined that I should go. I won the battle in the end but it was a close-run thing and I believe that it was my mother's poor state of health that saved the day.

Finally, I was selected to be Training Major to the 4th Battalion, The Oxfordshire and Buckinghamshire Light Infantry (Territorial Army) in Oxford. I was delighted with this posting as I had a lot of friends in Oxfordshire and my Commanding Officer was to be Lieutenant-Colonel Peter Fleming, well known to me in my days in Delhi after the war, and with a considerable reputation as an author and traveller.

Peter and I became great friends and a lot of our Territorial Army business was done at his beautiful home, Merrimoles in Nettlebed, where I also got to know his charming wife (the late Celia Johnson, the famous actress). These were happy days, Fergus Higgins commanded the depot and I lived in the Cowley Mess.

The work was not difficult and I had to prepare interesting and exciting exercises for the Battalions' weekend training.

I had derived enormous benefits from my time as an instructor at the School of Infantry and I believe the Officers were well satisfied with their training.

Peter Fleming was an unorthodox soldier having served some time with Wingate in Burma and undercover operations in Greece and Crete, and Higher Authority and Brigadier Dicky Bird the Brigade Commander were continually 'bellyaching' at me to control him in some of our rather 'hare-brained' exercises.

One incident remains with me over the years; we were at a Territorial Army Camp at Fylingdales near Scarborough and on the first day at Camp Peter and I walked around to see what was happening. The band was playing and there was indescribable confusion in every department and Peter went back to his tent and composed a fourth leader for *The Times* describing a first morning in a Territorial Army Camp - it was hilariously funny.

It was there in *The Times* the next day and all hell was let loose. The War Office rang both Brigadier Dicky Bird and myself and we were reprimanded for not controlling Peter Fleming, but as I said to the Brigadier afterwards, how do you control someone as well known and important as him?

I hardly ever dined in the Depot Mess for I had a great many friends in the Oxford area. To name a few, Dick and Gosh Troughton (now Sir Charles and Lady Troughton) were particularly good to me and I spent enjoyable weekends at their lovely home, Wooleys, Hambledon; Pat Rathcredan who was my lawyer for a period, Colin and Anne Mackenzie (Colin was a Company Commander in 4th Battalion), Mr. and Mrs. John Clarke-Brown at Kingston Blount and many others.

Chapter 11

1953–1991 – Marriage – Life in Wensleydale – Territorial Army Service as Officer Commanding 4th Green Howards, (T.A.)

Colonel Graham Montague-Jones, a Company Commander in the 4th Battalion Oxf. and Bucks Lt. Infty (T.A.) advised on the setting up of a small business at Spennithorne previous to my retirement and his firm has run the accounting side for thirty years.

I had a considerable amount of time on my hands and with a view to retirement in the future I used to go and study organic gardening with cloches with an elderly Admiral who lived on the outskirts of Oxford. In addition to this, I visited the Art School of the Ashmoleum during my lunch break and made quite a lot of progress in watercolour painting which sadly I gave up when I left Oxford.

My last Territorial Army Camp with the 4th Battalion was in Norfolk and it was a great success as I had prepared some really exciting field firing exercises for the boys. At the final guest night, which was attended by the Colonel of the Regiment, General Sir Bernard Paget, Peter Fleming made a very nice speech on saying farewell to me and I was presented with a lovely silver salver. The next day I had a long session with Sir Bernard who begged me to change my mind and to go out to the British Army of the Rhine and to be Second-in-Command to Colonel Peter Young who was then commanding the Regiment. I said 'No' quite firmly as I had made a pension, albeit very small, but I wanted a life at Spennithorne and had ideas for the future.

It was in 1953 that I finally left the army, it had been a very full life and despite initial doubts I looked back on a career full of interest, excitement and enjoyment.

My mother and my aunt Ruth had looked after the Spennithorne Estate, not only throughout the War years, but also during the whole of my Army service and this was a very considerable achievement for two elderly ladies. After my sessions with the Admiral in Oxford I had learnt a fair amount about cloche gardening and I was determined to try and convert the Spennithorne Gardens into a commercial concern - I spent a great deal of money on cloches, greenhouses, cultivators and plants. In addition I took on a full-time gardener with experience in commercial gardening.

I made many mistakes, the layout of the old gardens could not be altered without totally spoiling the whole set-up, so this involved an unsatisfactory compromise resulting in an enterprise which was only partially successful. The weather in the Yorkshire Dales is extreme and the Spennithorne Gardens took a tremendous battering in Winter months over the years. The wastage in broken glass was enormous and financially crippling. I had no idea of marketing my produce or of prices and the greengrocer with whom I did business in Leyburn Market, when looking at my new Lettuce crates inscribed with my name, said, 'Well, these won't cut much ice with the Trade'. Rather discouraging, I thought. I decided after two years of struggle to reduce the market garden enterprise and try something else.

In my early life as these pages will have shown, my most endearing pastime and pleasure was cricket and I had promised Spennithorne sports enthusiasts that I would, when the war was over, give a few acres of Mill Flatts meadow below Spennithorne House for a permanent cricket ground. This ambition was achieved and cricket has thrived in Spennithorne for some fifty years. Henry and I played for the village many times and Tommy Stelling, a Spennithorne butcher and proprietor of the Old Horn Inn, was wicket keeper and captain.

The wickets in the Dales villages were pretty rough and on one occasion I had my little finger broken by a rising ball from a quickish bowler; Tommy Stelling offered to hammer it straight with his butcher tools but I said 'No' and it is crooked to this day!

In addition to village cricket, I was still playing the Regimental Cricket Week at Oxford and occasionally for the I Zingari and Free Foresters. One game I recall with great enjoyment was for the I Zingari against Sir

Leonard Hutton's XI played on the late Sir William Worsley's lovely ground at Hovingham.

It was 1954 and I was 43 and although I had had many girlfriends it was never guite right for either them or me. Imogen was the daughter of Major General Walter Clutterbuck of Hornby Castle, Bedale, eight miles from Spennithorne. I had known Walter for years but it was only after my retirement from the Army that Imogen and I got to know each other. It was a very short courtship and we both knew that it was totally 'right' for both of us. We were married in Hornby Church in May 1954. My marriage to Im was a great success story, and she was a wonderful wife to me. She accompanied me always in all the activities connected with Politics and the Territorial Army and gave me great help in running my business.

In 1956 Henrietta was born and two years later Joanna came along. These daughters were a great joy to us.

By now I had decided to supplement the market garden with a modest investment in deep litter poultry and a small Jersey herd of about sixteen cows. Neither of these enterprises ever proved great money spinners but the Jersey herd, which was mainly Imogen's concern, gave us both much enjoyment and pleasure. Frankly, I really loathed the deep litter poultry. It was a never-ending job feeding them. The feed sacks were heavy and somehow the hens did not seem at all thankful for the food which I was forever giving them! Coccidiosis and feather pecking were just two of the horrible disorders with which these creatures were constantly afflicted – I believe that the depression which I suffered and which I mention later was in part due to these hens!

To complete my small business, I decided in 1959 to start a site for touring caravans in a disused quarry at Harmby. I owned a small area of this quarry and I was fortunate through my great friend, Tom Wrightson, to purchase the remaining area of the quarry from the Wyvill Estate nearby. There were many problems in the early days for I was in constant conflict with a neighbour who was also starting a caravan site in an area of the quarry not owned by me.

We had many differences over boundaries and a 'right of way' argument which lasted about fifteen years, finally ending in court action with the verdict in my favour.

My Caravan Park Warden in those early days was Mr. Tommy Young who, together with his wife Blanche, lived in a charming cottage close to the Park; they have been friends of mine for over thirty years and still operate a small select site near their cottage on my behalf.

By 1970 the Caravan Park was becoming a viable enterprise and I had been given enormous help and advice by the then Director General of the Caravan Club, Mr. Donald Chidson. In 1971 Donald was instrumental in recommending to me a full-time Warden, Mr. Tom East, who, with his wife Lilian, remained with me for thirteen years during which time we had achieved considerable success.

In 1974, I decided to enter into an agreement with the Caravan Club whereby the organization and day-to-day running of the Site should be the responsibility of the Club with a Warden chosen by the Club. After the annual expenses I would receive 85 per cent of the profit and these arrangements worked reasonably well until 1984 when the wind of change started to blow in a big way.

A new Director General of the Caravan Club was appointed with a somewhat inflexible Sites Committee and to put it mildly life with the Club became extremely difficult.

The Lease between myself and the Club, due to terminate in 1997, made NO provision for any capital expenditure and by the year 1984 both the Club and myself agreed that very considerable capital funding was necessary to bring the Site to a FOUR 'A' Standing.

Since 1984, I myself have contributed a considerable sum of money on capital improvements but both I and my daughters Henrietta and Joanna are extremely reluctant to provide further capital funding in the future.

There the matter stands in January 1991 and hopefully some satisfactory solution can be found between the Club and ourselves when we meet together shortly.

During the years 1988–1990 I was fortunate to be provided by the Club with another excellent Site Warden – Neville Prince and his wife Maureen were not only great friends to me but were also highly efficient.

In 1955 an old friend in the War years in Burma, the late Colonel Jonathan Forbes, who was then commanding the 4th Battalion The Green Howards T.A., suggested that I might like to come as his Second-in-Command with a view to taking over command when he finished his term of office.

This was a difficult decision to make as I already had many other commitments, nevertheless I regarded it as a great honour that this fine old County Regiment should select me, not even a member of the Regiment, for this command and I gladly accepted the appointment. An added incentive was that one of my illustrious ancestors had commanded the Loyal Dales Volunteers in Napoleonic times, these volunteers being the forerunners of the present Territorial Army Battalion of Green Howards. My previous experience of being a training Major in the 4th Battalion of the Oxf. Bucks (T.A.) with Peter Fleming was very useful to me and in the few months I had as Second-in-Command I was able to get to know all the Officers and many of the other ranks before taking over command from Colonel Forbes. I had two great allies in the Green Howards, Major General A. E. Robinson, the Colonel of the Green Howards, and Colonel Norman Littleboy, the Hon. Colonel of the 4th Battalion, who both helped and advised me in early days.

These early days were difficult as we had a Brigadier who was ambitious, was frightened of higher authority and was forever finding petty faults in all of his three Battalions of the Brigade. Together with the two other Commanding Officers in the Brigade, Oscar Norman of the Durham Light Infantry and Duggie Nixon of the East Yorks, we maintained a United Front against irksome and pin-pricking frustrations and in any case, I, as a Territorial Army Commanding Officer, was almost untouchable and was well placed to ignore these tiresome and trivial bellyaches with impunity.

The Territorial Army Drill Halls in North Yorkshire were all a long way from Spennithorne and Battalion H.Q. at Guisborough was forty-five miles away and I found myself in the early days doing this journey three times a week. At that time we had about 1,000 National Servicemen doing their three years' compulsory service and I found that I was working harder than at any time since the War.

Imogen was very good about accompanying me to the many social occasions and one I recall clearly was, when pregnant at a Green Howards dinner at Guisborough, she whispered to me that she was going to faint. Colonel Conyers Scrope, Commanding Officer of the 1st Battalion, was in the middle of a long speech but I felt that I must take her away as quickly as possible. We struggled out with the astonished glances of the guests and Colonel Conyers Scrope with commendable imperturbability, and never wavering for one instant, continued his speech to the end and Imogen and I made our way home.

I recall another incident which happened when I was in command of 4 Green Howards. I, and my Training Major, Tony Steed, had organized a River Crossing Exercise whereby we planned for the Battalion to cross the River Yore in assault boats at a point called the Beggars Mouth below Spennithorne village, the object being to capture Middleham Castle.

We had organized a terrific firework display of rockets and Very lights and the night was made hideous with bangs and explosions of every description. Alas, I had forgotten the effect this might have on the racehorses in Middleham and there was pandemonium in the many Middleham stables.

My old friend Neville Crump and many of the other trainers were furious and Neville actually paid me a visit at 3.00 a.m. in the morning to vent his rage.

Complaints were made to Higher Authority and the War Office but in those days the Territorial Army was considered more important than racehorses and I received no reprimand.

My period of command of 4 Green Howards lasted four years. The Battalion provided a guard of honour for Her Majesty the Queen when she visited Teesside in 1956 and Imogen and I were introduced to her – a great occasion – I subsequently became the Deputy Brigade Commander of 151 Brigade T.A. for four years to 1964 when I finally retired from all T.A. commitments. During my final year in the T.A., Tony Read (then a Major General commanding 50th Northumbrian Division Territorial Army) came to live in Thorney Hall, Spennithorne, very close to my own house so our paths crossed once again.

I had enjoyed tremendously good health throughout all my life but in 1958 I was smitten with a sinister and little-known malady. Certainly frequent visits and advice from a number of doctors failed to find a reason for my plight. Almost total lack of sleep and a lack of interest in anything were the symptoms. At this time I was heavily involved in a number of activities and in addition to Spennithorne Enterprises (Farm – Market Gardens and Caravan Park) I was Chairman of the Wensleydale School, a Deputy Lieutenant for North Yorkshire, a Justice of the Peace and Commanding Officer of 4th Battalion the Green Howards T.A. Matters came to a head when I had planned to organise and command an exercise in the Middlesborough area. I left Spennithorne for Guisborough that day feeling 'at a low ebb', but that somehow, I felt I must go through with this exercise which I had planned so carefully. I was fortunate to have some kind friends, George and Peggy Jenyns at Guisborough with whom I always stayed when the Territorial Army were operating in that area. I said to George and Peggy on arrival at Guisborough, 'I can't go through with this exercise, I feel bloody awful'. They were wonderfully kind and immediately called their own doctor Rex Belas, who incidentally was also well known to me as Medical Officer for 4th Green Howards, to come and see me. It was fortunate that Rex specialized in psychiatric disorders and he diagnosed a massive depression. Within a week I was under the care of a leading London psychiatrist, Mr. Morgan Witteridge, who prescribed E.C.T. and this treatment was carried out in Sister Agnes's Nursing Home in London and was entirely successful.

This episode in my life was very upsetting to Imogen as on a number of occasions I left home in the hope, I suppose, of achieving a cure by a change of scenery, first with my brother and Angela at Bracknell and then with Peter and Celia Fleming at Nettlebed. The early mornings were the worst and on one occasion, feeling that I was not doing enough to justify my existence, I answered an advertisement from a soft drinks firm to drive a wagon and carry out delivery of soft drinks! I received a very civil reply which indicated that I was considered not quite suitable for this particular type of work.

Towards the end of each day, however, my morale and spirits rose to such an extent that on another occasion I applied for the appointment of Chief Constable of the North Riding of Yorkshire where a vacancy existed but, I think rather fortunately, I was not accepted although I believe I reached the shortlist.

Sport played a big part in my life during the 1960s and 1980s – Henry and I were fortunate to have been able to rent Skelton Moor (Telfit and Moorhouse Farms) in the Marske area. These beautiful moors are owned by William Allison (Telfit) and Terry Allison (Moorhouse) and our families have enjoyed a close friendship for some twenty-five years. Annual grouse bags have been extraordinarily consistent and in 1988 we achieved a record bag of seventy-seven brace on 20th August.

In 1989 I held a party at Spennithorne House to celebrate the twenty-fifth anniversary of a happy association with my landlords William and Terry Allison at which all our families and friends were included.

For some years, I rented a small pheasant shoot at Thorney Farm, Spennithorne, which was great fun as a family shoot but many friends in North Yorkshire gave me splendid days pheasant shooting over the years.

Another source of great enjoyment for myself and my friends has been a duck flighting pond, named the Brickfield. It is situated about half a mile away near to the river Yore. My game book shows that we have been shooting this pond for thirty years about five times a year. This is a most exciting evening's entertainment for the shooters and their dogs.

In the years from 1960 onwards my father-in-law General Walter Clutterbuck gave us delightful holidays on Deeside and Imogen and I both learnt our salmon fishing from him. Henrietta and Joanna were always with us on these Scottish holidays and greatly loved Deeside.

Walter Clutterbuck, Imogen and I went for a holiday in Madeira in 1970. We liked it so much that we decided to build a villa on the seafront at Garajau, four miles from the main town of Funchal. This investment has been a great success and we have spent many happy Winter holidays on this lovely semi-tropical island.

I have already mentioned the Caravan Park at Harmby and close by, and included in the original purchase from the Wyvill Estate, was a quarry pool of about two acres. Tests showed that the water supply from a spring was ideal for trout and so it proved and for many years I and my friends have enjoyed some excellent sport from a small boat moored up in a cave on the edge of the pool.

The pool itself, surrounded by steep cliffs rising sheer from the water, appears rather grim and forbidding particularly in overcast weather, but lush vegetation and a profusion of flora and fauna round the water edges is a great attraction to both naturalists and Nature Conservancy.

It was in 1975 that misfortune befell my family and my younger daughter Joanna, aged only sixteen, suffered a massive stomach haemorrhage. She was quickly taken to the Radcliffe Infirmary in Oxford where no less than three operations were performed before the cause of the bleeding was found and finally stopped. Joanna nearly died but being young she recovered fairly fast. These were traumatic days for Imogen and myself and we spent the days with my brother and sister-in-law at Bracknell (who could not have been more caring for us) and at the Radcliffe with Jo. Shortly after, Imogen and I went for a holiday in Madeira and it was there that she noticed a small swelling in a gland in her neck later diagnosed as cancer. She had an operation to remove it and then the deep-ray treatment to follow which was an unpleasant experience. I used to visit her in the cancer hospital at Cuckfield near Leeds, but it was a depressing time and on many occasions she felt too ill even to talk to me. She recovered but sadly only temporarily. To add to these calamities, my mother-in-law, Gwen Clutterbuck, died after a short illness.

The early 1970s were not without interest, there were only forty acres of farmland immediately around the house so Imogen and I decided to buy two small farms, East Witton Lodge Farm, close to East Witton village and Busks Farm, near Middleham. This has been a very worthwhile investment and we have enjoyed good relations with our tenant farmers, William Allison and Michael Pickard.

In the 1980s I made a modest investment in forestry, purchasing two plantations on Witton Fell some four miles from Spennithorne. Prospects for capital appreciation in the future are good and my daughters should benefit substantially in twenty years' time.

From 1955 onwards I was involved in many local activities, these included being appointed a Justice of the Peace for the Hang West Division of North Yorkshire (this being the ancient title). I held this office for twenty-seven years, time consuming but well worthwhile; poaching was one of the main offences with which we had to deal and our reputation for stern sentences for this offence was legendary. In 1959 I was made a Deputy Lieutenant for the North Riding of Yorkshire and was required to represent the Lord Lieutenant on a number of occasions, the main ones being the funeral of the late Bishop of Birmingham, the Right Reverend Leonard Wilson, famous for his work whilst a prisoner of war in Japanese hands – I performed Deputy Lieutenant duties at the Great Yorkshire Show during Her Majesty the Queen's visit in her Jubilee year.

I became Chairman of the Richmond Division of the Conservative Party in 1965. This was a rewarding experience and Imogen and I attended Conservative Conferences at Blackpool and Brighton.

In 1970, I was persuaded by my friends to stand as County Councillor for Leyburn District and I was fortunate to be unopposed for my first term of office. In the next Election in 1973, I was opposed by a lady called Veronica Anderton Webster, but I managed to defeat her by a substantial number of votes. In 1977, I was again unopposed and in 1981, my adversary was a lady called Mrs Olive Turner whom I managed to defeat but with a reduced majority.

Those fifteen years on the North Yorkshire County Council were really happy ones when I got to know and understand the workings of local government and an insight into the enormous workload carried by the civil servants who administer the County.

During the early days, the late Bob Wotherspoon was the Chief Executive and later John Evans, both always gave me helpful and friendly advice.

The main committees on which I served were County Planning, Police and The Yorkshire Dales National Park – of these, The Yorkshire Dales

National Park Committee was to me the most important and most enjoyable. I was elected Chairman in 1973 and held this post until I resigned after seven years in office.

Our headquarters were at Bainbridge, in the middle of the National Park, and many of our meetings for planning and other matters took us to the remote corners of these lovely Dales. I like to feel that many of the rights of way which had become closed through neglect were reopened during the years that I was Chairman.

I made many friends on this Committee both among the Committee members and the National Parks Officers, Mr. Richard Harvey and his Assistant, Mr. George Hallas, who were always at hand to give their professional advice on our many and often difficult problems.

Imogen had been clear of her cancer troubles after her treatment in 1975 but in November 1979 it was diagnosed once again. We planned for her to stay with her sister Hope (Hops) in Chelsea Park Gardens in London and to go to the Royal Marsden Hospital (for cancer patients) when it was necessary.

This was a difficult time for me; I had commitments here, County Council work and other matters, so we decided together that I should come to London every ten days. There must be many people who are and have gone through the weeks of waiting and hoping that somehow a cure could be found, but it was not to be and Im died after a seven months' battle to survive.

I was much older than Imogen and we had consequently made plans for what should happen on my death. In 1970 we had built a new house (Lower Garden House) which she would have occupied after I had gone, but of course all these plans had to be altered. Lower Garden House is now let to my now great friends Sir Leon and Lady Brittan and I have every hope that they will remain there.

There must be thousands like me who, after a family disaster, wonder how to make the best of things; I thought of leaving Spennithorne for a small house, going on a world cruise, having a live-in lady either thirty years younger or the same age!

I pondered on all of these alternatives and discarded the lot – what I do know, however, is the enormous kindness and support that I have been given by my close friends. In the ten years since Imogen's death there is hardly a week gone by that I have not dined with Helen Wrightson and her late husband, Tom, and with Tommy and Sheila Pitman; Dame Margot Smith who lives close to me in the village has also been very supportive over the years, and I have been entertained by the late Captain Dick Scrope and his charming daughter, Elizabeth, for tea at their home in Middleham every week for many years.

I found the months after Imogen's death particularly difficult, so it was with great pleasure I accepted an invitation from the Wrightsons to go with them on a motor tour of Europe. They had compiled an exciting and attractive itinerary, and in early June 1982 we crossed the English Channel on a car ferry from Dover to Ostend. After an afternoon sightseeing and browsing round Brussels, we spent the first night in the train *en route* to Villach in Austria. Not a very comfortable night, the three of us in a four-berth couchette compartment, but I managed to oversleep, for which Tom and Helen didn't forgive me, as they had spent the night trying to keep other people from occupying our fourth bunk and listening to my snores, and were doubly aggrieved I missed the beautiful scenery in the morning! From Villach we drove to the small village of Fellbach in the Drau valley. There we spent a peaceful and enjoyable two days and received lavish hospitality from wartime friends of Tom's. I remember drinking Schnapps pretty heavily and recalling with nostalgia the occasion when thirty years previously the skipper of a Dutch boat in the Indian ocean was my undoing with the selfsame Schnapps.

From Fellbach we drove over the Monte Croce pass to Udine in Italy. We stayed at Lake Garda where it poured with rain and we couldn't see the lake.

Venice was our next port of call and we stayed at a very attractive hotel on the Grand Canal, and during our two days' visit, we managed to see most of the spectacular buildings of this beautiful city.

I remember a long, hot and tiring drive from Venice to Ravenna, but we were fortunate to come upon a delightful hotel high above the sea where we consumed many gins and tonic and enjoyed the wonderful view.

It was now the eighth day and we arrived at Sienna where the Palio was in progress, this was a most entertaining and spectacular display. On the following day we visited Monte Casino, almost completely demolished during World War II and now wonderfully restored almost to its former splendour.

Our tenth night in Matera (in Southern Italy) was not a success: It was frightfully hot, a firework display was in progress throughout the night and I found the coolest place was a chair on the hotel landing.

The next day we crossed on the ferry from Brindisi to Corfu where we spent a most enjoyable and restful seven days in the Wrightson's delightful villa.

After our Corfu holiday we boarded the ferry to Ancona (Italy) and then drove to Urbino, spending two nights in an old country house with a lovely fruit orchard. I met a very nice Englishman and we had long chats in the garden about cricket and found we had much in common. Tom and Helen took their visit to the Ducal Palace very seriously. Finally we drove on the fast motorway from Pesaro-Milan, boarded the train from Milan-Brussels where we had an enormous lunch and thence (rather too replete) to the ferry Ostend/Dover to finish a memorable holiday.

The success and enjoyment of my travels in Austria and Italy encouraged me to go for fresh fields in 1983 – this time it was to join a party ('Art Study Tours') which was organized by two ladies, Pamela Nicholson and Gail Jopling, both charming and very efficient.

The destination was the Soviet Union and the party mainly consisted of Yorkshire folk. We left Heathrow on May 11th in an Aeroflot aircraft bound for Moscow. The flight was uneventful but I recall a long delay at Moscow Airport where Baggage–Passports took much longer than in the U.K.

We were booked into the Moscow National Hotel and almost immediately walked across to Red Square where we saw the changing of the Guard at Lenin's Tomb – Red Square was packed with people and, trying to be helpful in keeping our party together, I tied a white handkerchief to my walking stick, raising it aloft for their guidance. Red Guards descended upon me and I was forced to capitulate and take my flag down – Red Square was most impressive and was floodlit on the evening we arrived.

Living conditions in Moscow were a bit austere. My bedroom was scrupulously clean but pretty basic. We were warned about a shortage of basin and bath plugs and told to take a reserve and sure enough I required one for my bath. There was a very clean loo, but sadly the pan was not fixed securely to the floor and I went round in a circle! No worry, it was all great fun. The National Hotel food was adequate but not spectacular and fruit and vegetables were in short supply.

The next day (May 12th) we visited the Pushkin Museum and saw an amazing collection of Impressionists' paintings – Monet – Manet – Renoir – Gauguin and many others. In the afternoon a city tour of gold-domed cathedrals within the Kremlin and in the evening to the Bolshoi Theatre to see Mussorgsky's opera *Khovanshchina* written in 1876 but set in 1610 with the wonderful sets of Red Square, real live horses on stage and an incredible 'fire' which destroyed one of the set buildings most convincingly! Three hundred people in the chorus and eighty in the Orchestra, an unforgettable and exciting evening.

May 13th – A visit to Zagorsk just after an Easter religious festival – we witnessed the annual blessing of the holy water, most moving, with orthodox Bishops in their finery.

On the 14th we lunched at Akhangelskoe and visited the Palace. A circus in the evening rather disappointing but the highlight was a journey home on the Metro when Sue Mountgarret somehow got carried away on her own but managed to rejoin us on a returning train – the escalators move faster in Russia so some care is required in their use.

The next two days we visited magnificent cathedrals at Gulovsky and Suzdal, this included an attractive walk of one and a half miles across water meadows covered with a profusion of dandelions forming a veritable yellow carpet.

We returned to Moscow on May 17th and took the night sleeper to Leningrad. I was impressed with the sleeping cars, they are more roomy than ours in the U.K. and I had a good night's sleep.

In Leningrad we were given an excellent Intourist guide called Tamara and started with a city tour after which a visit to the Hermitage where we saw a notable array of fabulous pictures and old Masters such as Rembrandts, the Malachite Room and intricate wooden inlaid floors.

We spent the next morning at Oranbaum, the only building complex to escape untouched in World War II, then a walk through the Park and a picnic lunch in glorious weather with a temperature of seventy degrees. That afternoon we visited Peterhof where the fountains of the Grand Cascade were being tested – a marvellous spectacle – and all appliances treated with 'gold leaf'.

In the evening we went to our second circus – a very spectacular performance where no less than eight tigers and eight lions appeared in the arena together; my seat was next to a gangway and I was somewhat startled to see a bull (horns and all) moving up the gangway — he passed within a few inches of me but appeared disinterested – I breathed again!

It was now May 19th and I remember a quietish day mainly of walking in Leningrad. There was a gala evening in the Hotel with the following menu – hard boiled eggs and caviar – blinis and sour cream – chicken Kiev and mashed potatoes – vodka – wine and champagne – all Russian fare. There was also dancing to a band.

May 20th was taken up visiting two museums, one of which used to be the town house of the mother of our tour guide Prince George Galitzine. We viewed lovely portraits by Sarov – that same evening to the theatre to see a performance of Morovian folk dancing.

Last day and we went to see the ballet *La Sylphide* at Maly Theatre – Sir Fitzroy and Lady Maclean were in the audience and we were introduced to them – a very enjoyable ending with a farewell dinner.

It had been a ten-day holiday packed with activity and excitement, superbly organized by Pamela Nicholson and Gail Jopling and accompanied by Prince George Galitzine, an expert on Russian history. We had seen many of the fabulous buildings and treasures of Russia and obtained a good idea of how the people of Russia live – not as comfortable or luxurious as we in the West, but nevertheless perhaps superior in some ways and one example being their cleanliness, that is to say practically no litter or refuse and the streets washed frequently. Being a Communist State there is stricter discipline and we were informed that muggings and street violence generally were almost unheard of.

A satisfied party took off by Aeroflot on the return flight bound for the U.K. on May 21st with many happy memories.

Over the years I have been blessed with a hardworking and efficient staff at Spennithorne.

Roy and Lorna Burton worked for me from 1958 to 1968. Those years were a high point for Spennithorne Enterprises and together we operated a Jersey herd, deep litter poultry and a market garden with considerable success.

Mrs. Frank Watson came to cook for my mother and myself from 1962 to 1965 after which she was joined by her husband, Frank, when both worked for me in the Garden from 1965 to 1972. This partnership gave excellent service for some seventeen years.

Mr. Fred Wilkinson, the present Gardener, has been with me for eleven years. His professional knowledge and hard work have restored the Rock and Kitchen Gardens to their former glory. He acted as part-time keeper for me for many years – he has been a loyal friend throughout my life.

Harry Taylor has recently joined us and is a most valuable member of the team both in the garden and on the Estate.

Mrs. Agnes Lumley has been with us at Spennithorne House for no less than thirty five years. Throughout this long period she has served my mother, my own and my brother's families and as a close friend of all of us she has given us indispensable and devoted service - a very special person.

For the first four years after Im's death I remained as a County Councillor and as Chairman of the Yorkshire Dales National Park Committee and with my other local commitments, the bench, Caravan Park and my Forestry operations, I was pretty fully employed.

There were also some trivial and lighthearted incidents during these years that relieved the tedium of living alone; the TV series, *All Creatures Great and Small* carried out scenes in both the house and gardens in 1985 and 1987. I appeared in *The Tatler* as one of the most eligible batchelors over 70. The result of this was that I was invited by the B.B.C. to be interviewed on television. I accepted reluctantly and bitterly regretted it as I was inundated with letters on every subject, including proposals of marriage.

It would be a grave omission from my story if I did not mention the close association I have had with Spennithorne Church throughout my life.

Memorials to many generations of my ancestors in stone and stained glass add beauty and lustre to a very beautiful building.

In my early life my brother Henry and I attended church every Sunday and on weekdays at family prayers before breakfast when the House Staff were present.

Alas, I cannot say now at an advanced age that everything worked smoothly in our church affairs - Spennithorne throughout most of my life was dominated by the squires (including myself) of the three large houses and there were often disagreements between us which rebounded upon the unfortunate rectors.

I also believe that our constant bickering and quarrels influenced the church hierarchy in the choice of rectors which in the main have NOT been to everyone's liking.

Choice of a rector is still in the hands of the squirarchy owning the living, in our case, squires of neighbouring villages, and this has always been a 'bone of contention' to me.

I sincerely believe that the appropriate church hierarchy should submit the names of possible candidates to the Chief Church Warden of the Parish concerned, who should then call a meeting of selected members of the P.C.C. for interview and selection and the period called the 'Interregnum', i.e. the interval between the retirement of the incumbent Rector and the installation of a new one normally lasting for several months, should be abolished and a proper handover to take place between the rectors concerned over a reasonable period of time.

My daughters, Henrietta and Joanna, have been a great comfort to me and we frequently visit each other in London and Spennithorne. My brother, Henry, and sister-in-law, Angela, have given me happy holidays in Scotland fishing on the Carron, and I have often enjoyed their hospitality at their Berkshire home.

Looking ahead, Henrietta, beautiful, but also firm and resolute, is being groomed to take over the Spennithorne Estate when I am gone. Behind her and in the wings are my grandson and granddaughter, Edward and Victoria, so the future seems assured.

In conclusion, I am justly proud of my family's great tradition of service with the Armed Forces of the Crown. In the past 150 years out of 35 males, 28 have served in the Army or the Navy - can these figures be surpassed by any other family in the United Kingdom?

It seems strange to the reader that, although endowed with many of the good things in life, a wealth of colourful and exciting memories to reflect on, an affectionate family and close friends readily accessible, that with all this I am not really very happy. It is a kind of Chestertonian paradox but living alone in an old house of considerable size, once so filled with the noise and laughter of a family growing up, can be depressing especially when visitors have come and gone, and particularly during the long Winter evenings and nights.

Even good health and material comforts do not compensate for basic loneliness and having had an Army life packed with friends and acquaintances and a wonderfully happy married life, I am singularly ill-equipped for a semi-solitary existence, and look to fate for some turnabout in whatever time may be left to me. With that hope and great appreciation for what has been given to me by way of ancestry, environment, good health and adventure, I now end this story.

APPENDIX

THE EAST AFRICAN CAMPAIGN, SOMALILAND AND ABYSSINIA

Order of the Day by Lt.-General Sir Alan Cunningham

To: 11 Div. 12 Div.
From Force Nairobi
Important

No. 19658 stop The following message from the Force Commander will be made known to all troops under your command stop Force Commander also directs that the operation and its scope should also now be explained to troops stop Begins stop The victories of Imperial troops further north have filled us in East Africa with pride and excitement though no doubt the ensuing period has been touched with envy and strong desire to emulate achievements stop Chance is now before you to prove what I well know that E.A. Force is no whit behind in dash courage and endurance stop In this confidence I send to South African East African West African and Indian troops taking part in operations a message of good luck stop Hit them Hit them hard and hit them again stop

Cunningham addressed 11 Div., 12 Div.

10th Feb. 1941. (Signed) J. Keith Edwards, B.G.S.

Order of the Day by Major General A. R. Godwin Austen C.B., O.B.E., M.C., commanding 12th African Division on May 10th 1941

For the past month, in appalling conditions of weather, you have been engaged in operations against the strongest and most stoutly held position yet encountered by us in the campaign. The enemy disposed his troops holding it skilfully in depth for the first time because he knew the ground well and had himself defied by Abyssinian forces there for almost a year.

Your first action was to attempt to discover the extent of the position and the manner in which it was held. This entailed numerous reconnaissances over extremely difficult country and many encounters by fighting patrols. Your hardihood in reconnaissance and courage in minor engagements were characteristic of your resolution. This activity cost you casualties which I was resolved should not, if possible, be incurred in vain.

Immediately therefore, you had located the best line of approach I ordered an attack on this very strong position, realising only too early what a call I was making on you. You were asked to advance through a forest so dense that the enemy was convinced it completely safeguarded his left flank.

My reason for asking you to attack was not to gain a purely local success. The war here has reached a stage in which the sooner we can dispose of the remaining elements of the Italian Army and hand over

Abyssinia to its ruler the Emperor, Haile Selassie, the sooner shall we be able to release to General Wavell the armament and transport he so sorely needs for bigger operations against the Germans. One of our earliest necessities to reduce the amount of transport required for maintenance in the clearance of a through road from Nairobi to Addis Ababa. You have just cleared that section of the best road which was most strongly held. You have thus won not a local but a strategic victory.

(Signed) A. R. Godwin Austen
Major General Comd. 12 African Division.

THE BURMA (KALADAN) CAMPAIGN
15th Indian Corps
Special Order of the Day by Lieut-Gen. Sir A. F. Philip Christison, K.B.E., C.B., M.C., Cmnd. 15th Indian Corps, 14th February, 1945.

To: 81 (West African) Division.

You have just completed an arduous campaign in some of the most difficult mountain jungle and chaung intersected country in the whole S.E.A. theatre.

You have built up a fine reputation as a Division since your entry into the theatre of operations, which began in December 1943 and ended with the capture of Myohaung, the ancient capital of Arakan, in January, 1945.

You have fought and defeated parts of 54 and 55 Japanese Divisions from Kaladan to the Kalapanzin. You have showed a fine fighting spirit. Aggressive and relentless in attack, you have learnt to defend skilfully, and to hold your fire and your ground when yourselves were attacked. I am very proud of you all and have specially asked that you may be retained under my command.

You had the unenviable role of drawing off from the main front the maximum possible of enemy forces in order so to weaken his Mayu and Akyab garrison that the latter place could be assaulted from the sea.

So successful were you that the Jap Command had to thin out his Akyab garrison piecemeal to stop your advance down the Kaladan, an advance which threatened his main L. of C. via Minbya for all his forces in Arakan.

He found himself finally with only one Bn. to defend Akyab, and concluding that this had little chance of achieving its object he pulled it out as we landed, again in order to try and stem your advance.

The fate of Akyab was sealed when you won the battle of Tinma and outflanked his Kauktaw positions.

I thank you for this fine contribution to the overall plan, and congratulate you all on your fine spirit and your successes.

You will I hope have a considerable period of rest and refitting ahead of you; I know I can rely on you to get the best out of this period and that you will maintain that high standard of discipline and correct relationship to the civil population for which you have also won a name.

I hope most of you will get and enjoy some leave, and I wish you a pleasant time and all good luck for the future.

(Signed) A. F. P. Christison, Lieut-Gen. Commanding.

Message received from the Supreme Allied Commander, South East Asia, 26th July, 1945.

Now that the operations in which you have been engaged in Burma have been so successfully completed and your return to your home country is imminent, I wish to acquaint all officers, N.C.O.s and men of 81st West African Division of my sincere appreciation and gratitude for their outstanding services in fighting for the liberation of Burma. From the commencement of your active operations in the Arakan in December, 1943, you have shown magnificent fighting qualities, both in your advance down the Kaladan valley in support of operations against Maungdaw and Buthidaung, and also in your determined battle through the jungles of the Kaladan in October, 1944. You have withstood and overcome the rigours of the 1944 monsoon in the upper Sangu valley day by day and established a reputation for your division which will always be remembered in the annals of the Burma campaign.

I wish you all the best of luck.

(Signed) Louis Mountbatten

Special Order of the Day by Major-General F. J. Loftus-Tottenham D.S.O., G.O.C. 81 (W.A.) Division, 27th January, 1945.

On successful conclusion of the Kaladan campaign I wish to thank all Commands, Staffs, and all ranks of every Department and service for the magnificent spirit they have shown.

The Division was by no means fresh when it set out on the vital task of clearing the last remaining threat to India's Frontier, what is more the advance unavoidably started at a bad period of the year.

In spite of those handicaps the cheerfulness, co-operation, and constant willingness to take on any operation, any time and any where, has been beyond all praise and shown equally by European and African. The endurance and bravery has been of an equally high order and the Division is now recognised as a First Rate Fighting Formation.

I feel that provided that we can maintain our present standards of Endurance and Leadership there is nothing that the Division cannot achieve and I am extremely proud of having commanded you through this campaign.

(Signed) F. J. Loftus-Tottenham, Maj-Gen.
Comd. 81 (W.A.) Div.

Glossary of Abbreviations

A.A.	Anti Aircraft
A/Cpl.	African Corporal
A.D.S.	Advanced Dressing Station
A.N.C.O.	African Non-Commissioned Officers
A.O.R.	African Other Rank
A/Tk.	Anti Tank
Aux. Gp.	Auxiliary Group
B/C.S.M.	British Company Sergeant Major
Bde.	Brigade
Bn.	Battalion
B.N.C.O.	British Non-Commissioned Officer
B/Sgt.	British Sergeant
Capt.	Captain
C.O.	Commanding Officer
Coy.	Company
Cpl.	Corporal
D.A.A.G.	Deputy Assistant Adjutant General
D.A.A. & Q.M.G.	Deputy Assistant Adjutant and Quartermaster General
Fd.	Field
hrs.	hours
i/c	in charge
L.M.G.	Light Machine Gun
Lt.-Col.	Lieutenant-Colonel

L/Cpl.	Lance Corporal
M.G.	Machine Gun
Maj. Gen.	Major General
N.R.	Nigeria Regiment
O.C.	Officer Commanding
O.O.	Operation Order
O.R.S.	Orderly Room Sergeant
Pl.	Platoon
Pte.	Private
R.E.	Royal Engineers
Recce	Reconnaissance
Regt.	Regiment
R.Q.M.S	Regimental Quartermaster's Sergeant
R.S.M.	Regimental Sergeant Major
Sgt.	Sergeant
u/c	under command

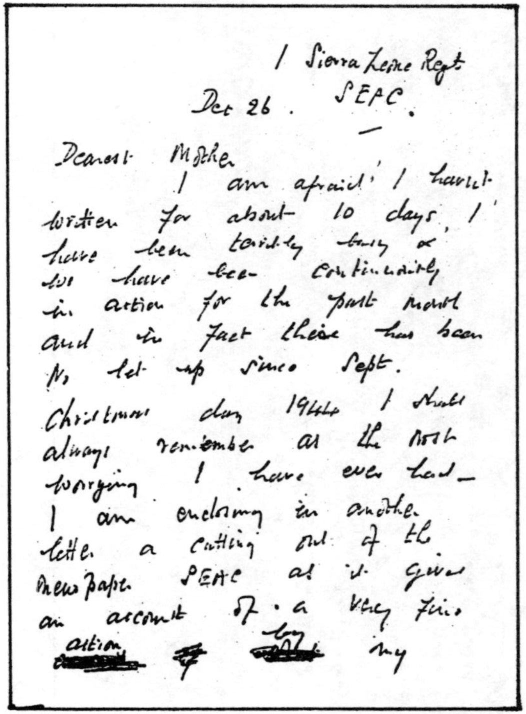

1 Sierra Leone Regt.
SEAC.

Dec 26.

Dearest Mother

I am afraid I haven't written for about 10 days, I have been terribly busy as we have been continually in action for the past month and in fact there has been no let up since Sept.

Christmas day 1944 I shall always remember as the most worrying I have ever had — I am enclosing in another letter a cutting out of the newspaper SEAC as it gives an account of a very fine action [redacted] ~~of~~ by [redacted] my

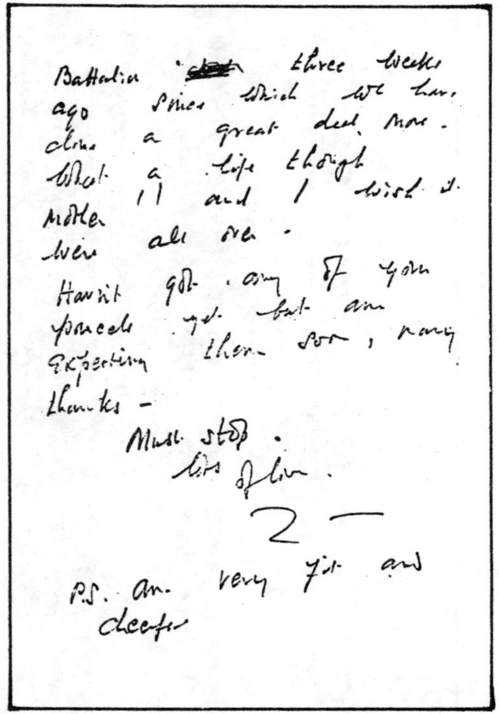

Battalion [redacted] three weeks ago since which we have done a great deal more. What a life though Mother!! and I wish it were all over.

Haven't got any of your parcels yet but am expecting them soon, many thanks —

Must stop.
Lots of love.

Z —

P.S. Am very fit and cheerful

3rd Bn Gold Coast Regt.
c/o A.P.O.
July 17th East Africa Force.

Dearest Mother
I havn't written you a decent letter for
sometime & I feel now that there can be no
harm in telling you where we have been
since I landed on 12th July last year.
Whether you have guessed or not I don't know
but up till Christmas last year we were
in WASIR this was a boring and soul
destroying existance as we were uncertain what
was going to happen. Several times during
these months we went to BUNA which relieved
monotony and was definitely too exciting.
As you know we went to EL WAK just
before Christmas and then had six weeks rest
at Mile 62 near Nairobi.
On January 26th we moved to the TANA
River near Garissa where we did some
specialized training for 10 days and on Feb
19th we started advancing I cannot give you
a full story of this but before the end
of the month we had captured AFMADU: after
this Tony's Battalion had a very fierce battle

at BURRO ERILLO and on Feb 20 we crossed the JUBA. A few days later we attacked and captured GELIB with an enormous number of prisoners and masses of stores.
From GELIB we moved very fast and captured BARDERA ISCAIA BAIDOA and LUGH FERANDI in all these places we captured a lot of prisoners and material.
We spent about 3 weeks in LUGH and Dolo and then went on to NEGHELLI (which I expect you have heard of) we had to fight for NEGHELLI although this was NOT a very difficult proposition.
We spent about 3 weeks in Negelli a very pleasant place and about the middle of April we moved north again.
By this time the Rains had started good and proper and it was bitterly cold. About 30 miles from Negelli at a place called UADARA we met the strongest opposition yet encountered. It is difficult to describe how this battle which lasted about 6 weeks and was very fierce, it was carried out in appalling weather conditions and was most unpleasant.
Since we captured the UADARA position, it has been

procession and we have moved fast many thousands of miles rounding up and capturing whole divisions of Wops.

I have been in ADDIS ABEBA during the last few days where I enjoyed myself a lot meeting many old friends including Ray Redman my greatest friend at Sandhurst and whom I once stayed with at Winchester. I also had lunch at the British Legation where I met Major General Sammy Butler who knew Pat very well and told me he nearly married her (I didn't tell him what a lucky man he was).

I don't know what the future holds for us I do NOT want to go back to the Coast which I gather is a possibility. I MAY be able to get out of it although in many ways I should be very sorry to leave the Gold Coast Regt. I have various schemes on hand all of which need very careful consideration made all the more difficult owing to the fact that I am still hoping for this Staff Course and if I do anything precipitous I may loose the opportunity, however if we move before the next course begins I shall NOT get the

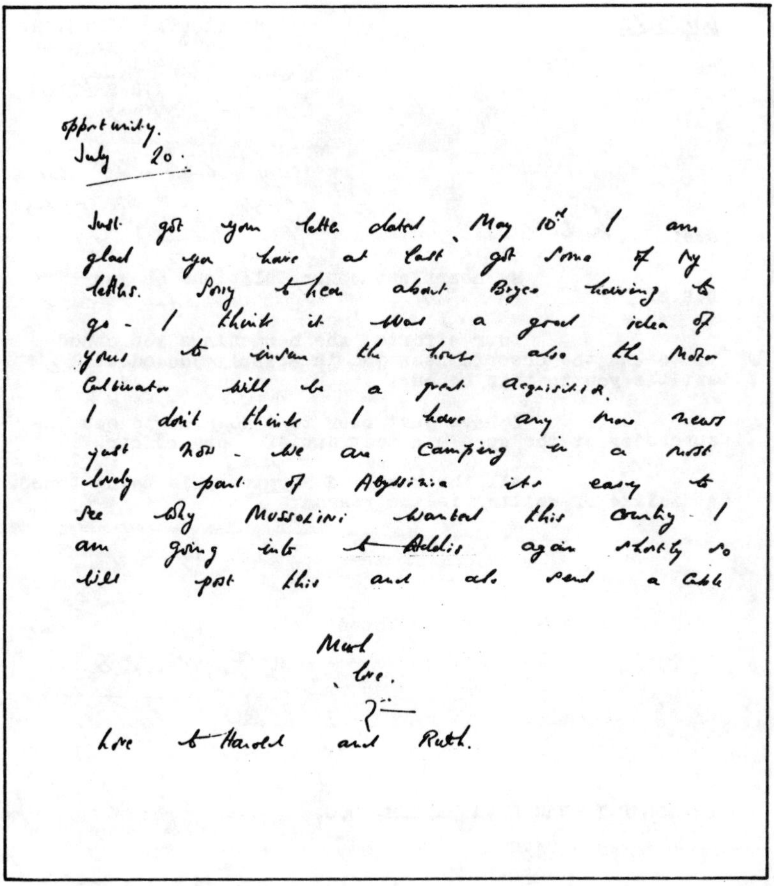

opportunity.
July 20.

Just got your letter dated May 10th I am glad you have at last got some of my letters. Sorry to hear about Bryce having to go - I think it was a great idea of yours to insure the house also the Motor Cultivator will be a great acquisition.
I don't think I have any more news just now - We are camping in a most lovely part of Abyssinia its easy to see why Mussolini wanted this country. I am going into ~~to~~ Addis again shortly so will post this and also send a cable

Much
love.

[illegible]

Love to Harold and Ruth.

From

Major General F.J.Loftus Tottenham, D.S.O.,

DO/451/G

HQ 81 (WA) DIVISION
ABPO 14

18 SEPT 45

Dear Philip,

My heartiest congratulations on your D.S.O.

Your efforts, the hammerings you stood up to and the cheerfulness you invariably showed well entitle you to this honour.

I have just been to SINGAPORE to see the surrender of the apes - a most satisfactory affair.

All the best and forgive this being typed, a dislike of writing is the reason.

Yours

Tottenham

LT-COL P.T. VAN STRAUBENZEE, DSO.

P.S Am delighted you have got the D.S.O.

This letter is one of my most treasured possessions.

The family coat of arms